Forbidden Games
& Video Poems

W9-BDW-441

Forbidden Games & Video Poems

The Poetry of
Yang Mu and Lo Ch'ing

Translation and commentary by
JOSEPH R. ALLEN

Property of
Diversity of thought
lending library

UNIVERSITY OF WASHINGTON PRESS
Seattle and London

This book was published with the assistance of grants from the Council for Cultural Planning and Development, Executive Yuan, Republic of China, and the Pacific Cultural Foundation, Taiwan.

Copyright © 1993 by the University of Washington Press
Printed in the United States of America

All rights reserved. No part of this publication may be reproduced or transmitted in any form, or by any means, electronic or mechanical, including photocopy, recording, or any information storage or retrieval system, without permission in writing from the publisher.

ISBN 0-295-97262-9 (cloth), 0-295-97263-7 (pbk.)

The paper used in this publication meets the minimum requirements of American National Standard for Information Sciences—Permanence of Paper for Printed Library Materials, ANSI A39.38-1984.

For sources of the poems translated in this volume, see pages 429–30.

Contents

Video Poems:
The Poetry of Lo Ch'ing   209

Acknowledgements

This all began in 1985 on a bus ride to the Taipei airport. We were two friends working our way through that awkward hour of parting with a casual conversation, a "wouldn't it be interesting" kind of digression. Wouldn't it be interesting for someone whose training was in classical Chinese poetry to write about contemporary poets and poems? We vaguely imagined an intellectual portrait of the Chinese poet in these near-postmodern times, set against the tradition of the poet in premodern China. And, yes, perhaps some translations as well: a little collection, just to round it all out. But when the idea came to pass, the translations began to overshadow the study, and this time the edges became the center.

That reconfigured project resulted in part from my good fortune of being funded in 1987–1988 by both a Fulbright Research Fellowship and a Language and Research Fellowship from the Inter-University Program and Academia Sinica in Taiwan. The first allowed me to live a year in Taipei and the second gave me access to the faculty and facilities of IUP (affectionately still known as the Stanford Center), where the project evolved into its present form. For a few months I led the ideal life. Early each morning I prepared the poems to be read and discussed (in Chinese) in classes that afternoon. After a late-afternoon bike ride through the hills around Taipei, I spent the evening trying to make the leap into English with rough translations of our afternoon readings. All to begin again the next morning. So the weeks went by and the poems became center to my life.

The poems translated here were selected in collaboration with the poets. I first asked Yang Mu and Lo Ch'ing each to select 150 of his favorite poems, with no criteria other than personal choice (neither poet had a selected works). Of the nearly three hundred poems, I translated (sometimes abortively) about half, and from those selected the poems presented here. I did not talk to the poets about the meaning or interpretation of any of their poems. In the end I chose translations that I thought worthy of the voices of the poets. I did not try to rewrite a given poem into its English version;

rather I tried to write the poem that I thought the poet might have written if he had written in English. That was the work that came to sustain me: trying to speak in their voices. In doing so I felt I was creating the poems themselves—the imperialism of translation.

From that bus ride to this final volume I have had many supporters and friends. First of all, Yang Mu and Lo Ch'ing helped in a multitude of ways, but especially by their generosity of spirit that allowed me to proceed blithely along massacring their art, pretending it was my own. Next were my two tutors at IUP, Chou Ch'ang-chen and Yang Chiu. Not only did they help keep me off the shoals of my own ignorance, they also provided tell-tales of how the poems sounded to a native reader. These two women are a writer's best audience: bright, widely read, articulate, and of open mind. Then there was my catalog of ships: student and friend Paula Fodor; Dr. Wu Jing-jyi, Tony Wang, and Amy Chou of the Taipei Fulbright office; my fellow Fulbrighters, especially Jerry Williams and Stephen Durrant; colleagues and readers Bill Matheson, Brett Millier, and Zhou Danlong; and Liu Shu-ling of Fu-jen University, who proofread the Chinese manuscript. I would also like to thank my friends at the University of Washington Press: Naomi Pascal, editor-in-chief; Veronica Seyd, production manager and designer of the book; and Lorri Hagman, who did double duty as copy editor and publicist—she even found the lost lawnmower. And always, of course, Lauren.

The bilingual publication of this book was made possible by a grant from the Council for Cultural Planning and Development, Executive Yuan, Taiwan, Republic of China, and brought to completion with a Pacific Cultural Foundation subsidy. The typesetting of the Chinese text was done by Meadea Enterprises of Taipei. A summer grant from Washington University Graduate School allowed me to complete the manuscript—my special thanks to Dean Edward N. Wilson. To all these friends and organizations, I am truly grateful.

Joseph R. Allen

Forbidden Games
& Video Poems

Written with People in Mind
Yang Mu

One winter morning two years ago I awoke to the sound of falling rain and to a bone-chilling dampness permeating my room. While I sat there in the cold thumbing through a book and drinking my tea, the noise of the city came to me woven into the patter of the rain; it grated on my nerves as it would occasionally drown out the rain altogether. Such was the morning traffic along Keelung Road, which runs north and south through the city of Taipei. But slowly my mind began to clear and my energy return. Putting the din of traffic out of mind, I took up a pen and wrote that somewhat unwieldy line "Someone asked me about truth and justice."*

In the last ten years modern Chinese poetry has undergone a number of noticeable changes. It seems to me that those changes have been limited to the mode of poetic expression and have not affected the actual concerns or intention of the literature itself. My understanding may differ some from that of my colleagues, but I believe that if we share basic aesthetic ideals, then it will not matter that we differ, or even completely disagree, on lesser points. I cannot imagine anything more deplorable than a society that marches in unison to a single drum—and if this is true for hairstyles and clothes, how much more should it be for the art of poetry. Mode of expression and point of view may change, but poetry's spiritual intent and cultural aims, its adherence to a transcendent aesthetic, and its concern with the quality of reality, all the while it adjudicates the infelicities of language and rhythm, cannot be compromised for the sake of mere politics or ideology.

Poetry is always made to live again by a renewal that rises

From the opening of "Written with People in Mind" (Shih wei jen erh tso), the postface to Yang's *Yu-jen* (Someone) volume of poems. This represents about two-thirds of the essay; the remainder is more concerned with the specifics of the poems of that volume.

*Translator's note: "Yu jen wen wo kung-li ho cheng-i te wen-t'i" is the refrain line and poem title I translate as "Someone Asked Me about Truth and Justice." For Yang Mu, it is a rather prosaic line.

from within. Torn down it rebounds; when things are worst it flourishes. Because it combines the power of immanence with that of transcendence, poetry is forever born anew.

Poetry holds firm; it affords no compromise.

I recall how all that morning while I worked on "Someone Asked Me about Truth and Justice," the rain continued, sometimes falling lightly, sometimes hard; yet the coldness of the room bothered me no longer and the noise of the city outside my window had lost its power to distract. Having written about two-thirds of the poem, I took it with me when I went to the university that afternoon. Coincidentally, that was the day of the final exam for my class in English poetry. I handed out the exam questions and took a seat at the desk in front of the room, where I pressed pen to paper again. In the midst of my muse, I would occasionally lift my head to look at the rows of students who worked diligently throughout the room: occasionally that sublime interweaving of grief and joy would suddenly shine forth in their faces. When the bell sounded, the students handed in their exams and I had completed the first draft of the poem.

This, of course, was an unusual situation in which to write. My students had no idea that while they worked diligently on their essays discussing Dryden and Pope, I sat in front of them absorbed in the task of writing a poem whose topic was the very feelings of their generation. That winter Taiwan had held a general election and Taipei City had selected a number of relatively bizarre legislators from its list of candidates. Among them was one fellow who had not long ago pulled off the largest business scam in the history of the island. After the election, an embittered student asked me whether I thought there was any truth or justice in the world. "Well, I believe there probably is," I said. But as I mumbled my answer I thought of how Lu Hsün, when asked by the wife of Hsiang Lin about the existence of a soul and hell, had muttered, "In theory, yes, there ought to be—but it isn't for certain."* I knew, however, that if I did not address those feelings of doubt, even if it were in the most indirect way, I might end up feeling uncomfortable with myself forever.

In the past I have seldom written this way. I have always felt

---

*Translator's note: This is from the opening pages of early twentieth-century prose writer Lu Hsün's short story "New Year's Sacrifice" (Chu fu).

4

that poetry should not come in response to a rush of emotion. Rather, poetic inspiration should arise in a process of cool and objective consideration; it should ferment slowly, with much attention to discipline and technique. When I now reread this poem, it does not strike me as overly angry or bitter; rather, some of the emotional charge of the poem is concealed in its language, such that what remains is essentially poetic—the sketch of a moment in the life of typical young man. While I do not actually know this person, neither is he a stranger; for we all have at one time been young and filled with such consuming skepticism.

Besides the poem "Someone Asked Me about Truth and Justice" and similar ones that were produced in response to some external situation or event, there are also in this collection the earlier "Moon over Pass Mountain" and "Troubled Travel," and the slightly later "Panjshir Valley." "Moon over Pass Mountain" was written in imitation of the classical poetic form of "historic reflection," while "Troubled Travel" was intended to recreate the spirit of Tu Fu's "Northern Trip" and Li Shang-yin's "Travels to the Outskirts"; yet they also at certain points explore my personal situation, colored by imagination.* "Panjshir Valley," on the other hand, was written after reading a dismaying newspaper article. In March of that year the occupying Soviet forces in Afghanistan had launched their spring offensive; the Panjshir Valley was overrun and the defending Afghan guerrillas were decimated. This brought to mind an old Afghan friend of whom I had long ago lost track. I have collected these poems under the section called "New Music Bureau Poems." Of course, such themes were never part of the conventional topics of early medieval Music Bureau poetry, yet since they were "written with events and not texts in mind,"** I wanted to suggest their affinity with the genre of New Music Bureau poetry.

I realize that my relatively impassioned labor is not what Po Chü-i called the poetry of social criticism, a poetry that expressed

---

*Translator's note: "Historic reflection" (*huai ku*) is a subgenre of classical Chinese poetry based on the contemplation of historic sites and events. Tu Fu (712–770) and Li Shang-yin (ca. 813–858) were major poets of the T'ang dynasty (618–906); these poems are examples of their travel poetry.

**Translator's note: This is how Po Chü-i (772–846) describes his "New Music Bureau Poems" in his preface to that collection, the poems in which are characterized by their social concerns.

with immediacy and clarity his reaction to current events. While I do not necessarily disregard that type of writing, I also hope that the traces of my life's enterprise contain that which might be considered a multilayered significance. When I read literary history, especially the works of the major poets, my first impression is always of how they were never engaged merely in one thing, but rather in many: besides the various poetic forms of lyric, song, and rhapsody, they also wrote essays, treatises, slim volumes on large issues; and there are also their annotations and exegeses, letters, prefaces, travel diaries, inscriptions, biographies, and funereal memorials: they even wrote novels, plays, and the like. This is the cause of envy and inspiration. A cultural life of such discipline, detail, and brilliance, a life of such rich complexity constantly stirs our admiration; at the same time it causes us to forever lament our own small existences. Encouraged by the limitless energy of these poets, we are ready to throw ourselves into the task. But I am humbled by my own limitations. Although I am relatively clear about what tools and skills are at my disposal and about what is within my range, still in the end it seems so limited. Nevertheless, I also know that I am not willing merely to muddle around within the easy range of the possible. We know that if one's artistic life is worth sustaining in its completeness, then we must seek its meaning in the processes of experimentation and breakthrough. This is especially true for poetry.

A Poem Is a Cat in One's Mind
Lo Ch'ing

1

Poetry has the eyes of a cat. It can look directly into the noonday sun, its gaze taking in the blaze that normally blinds. At the same time it can look into the imponderable dark, its gaze penetrating that blackness, eyeing all that moves within.

2

On the outside, every poem should have its own design, but that design should emerge from its interior. The design might be monochrome or multicolored; it can even be a design without design, but the structure should coordinate its head, four limbs, and tail; each muscle and bone should be drawn together, rendering them inseparable. The pattern of the design is usually surprisingly innovative—once seen, it stays in one's mind. Owing to the unique characteristics of its markings, the inherent qualities of each cat are entirely manifested to the reader.

3

Color that is applied like rouge to hard surfaces will not stand the test of time: before long it will begin to fade and disappear. Overly elaborate rhetoric and other cosmetic treatments are perhaps necessary for paper cats or cats made of other artificial materials, but for real cats there is no need for decoration.

4

Confucius said, "Only when ornament and substance are duly blended do you get a true gentleman." This can be said of a cat too, and of poetry. Ornament is its markings and form, substance is its content and spirit. When the two are drawn together without distinction, then you have art.

From *Shih-jen chih teng* (The poet's lamp), 23–30.

7

5

A dog cannot suddenly leap out from a pack of cats and declaim madly, "Substantially I am really a cat, there has just been some mistake as far as my external form is concerned."

6

To fiddle with the language of a poem when the content itself is not clear is always a minor distraction; it does not strike to the heart of the matter. Content determines form, and form allows the content to be entirely exposed. Special content relies on a special form that is coordinated with it; when blended together they then reach their most complete expression.

7

Poetry is a cat crouched in one's mind ready to spring. Everyone owns one, but they are not often let out of the house to prowl. Some cats recognize their own kind when they meet and can get together for a tête-à-tête. Others, however, keep their distance and merely eye each other from afar. And there are others who have been shut in so long they don't even know they are cats.

8

Poetry is a cat that springs out of one's mind. Crouching in places where one would never expect to find it, it waits patiently in silence, the language of its whole body echoing itself, flesh and bones, hair and skin in perfect balance and harmony. It looks as if it merely were sitting there idly, but in fact every inch of its body, every bone and muscle is ready and waiting.

The reader must scrutinize each one carefully, trying to become one with it. He must analyze the twitch of its ears, the slap of its tail, and even the subtle changes in the markings of its body. If he does so, then he will know the secrets of its heart.

9

Often a poet surprises a reader with a poem that seems to sit there doing nothing, in a completely inconspicuous place. But once our curiosity is piqued, we begin to wonder. Why is that cat crouching there like that? What is its purpose? Is there something in the area that is changed or gains new significance because of it's being there?

10

Some poets have only one cat at their disposal that they keep putting in different places; others have a plethora of different kinds that they distribute around in various settings.

11

A poem is a cat whose whole body is ready and waiting, crouching there, looking intently at one and only one thing, its prey. That thing, that prey, is what the poet hopes to grasp, or perhaps have his reader grasp.

12

The climax of the poem is in that instant when its language, ready and aimed, strikes out. At that moment, the beat of its heart and the rhythm of its breathing are timed to that consummate movement. All its strength and speed are embodied in it, ready to fire.

13

A cat's prey is also a poet's prey, and vice versa. The relationship between the two is extremely subtle; sometimes it is the cat who leads the poet on, sometimes it is the poet who seduces the cat. Yet sometimes, without any plan or forethought, they end up supporting each other in their individual pursuits.

14

Some poets show the reader only the cat itself, never revealing its intended prey. Others cover the cat with various signs (some clear, some obscure) that lead the reader to discover what the prey is. Then there are others who promptly bind the cat and its prey together with ropes, while others, in their haste, simply drag the prey out and drop it into the reader's arms, forgetting completely about the cat.

15

A cat can catch mice, but that certainly is not all it does. It can also play with a ball, catch a butterfly, or even chase its own tail.

A truly healthy cat will not do just one thing, but neither will it do something that is beyond its basic nature. A cat has a lot in common with other animals, but also much that is not.

A cat has no overriding ambition to supplant the other animals. It is regretful that some poets cannot see this.

16

Some people are experts at reform, and they have reformed their cats. They have reformed ordinary cats into expert mouse-trapping cats. (But such cats are actually only mousetraps, not real cats.)

And they have gone so far as to create cats for trapping white mice and cats for trapping black mice. (These are, in fact, nothing more than mousetraps with major design flaws.) They pit these two types of mousetraps against each other, and finding pleasure in this, they crown themselves King of the Cats. That done, they then start a campaign to slaughter off the cats that are not machine-made.

17

These are mad times of mechanical cats; there are some that are actually barking like dogs. And what is more, one constantly hears the calls of tigers, leopards, hyenas, and the like.

But no matter what calls one hears, he need only listen closely to tell they are the sounds of machines.

18

In fact there are many types of prey and to be successful each requires a different kind of predator; one should not force a cat to the wrong task. If you insist on using a cat, then the results will usually cost you; not only will you harm the cat, you won't get your prey either.

1984

Yang Mu and Lo Ch'ing: A Profile
Joseph R. Allen

Men, especially Chinese men, are often revisions of their mothers. I first met the mother of Yang Mu in Hua-lien, Taiwan, in 1978. She was a delicate and gracious woman: small, slim, speaking to me in a lilting Japanese (because I did not understand her Chinese dialect). She did not speak much, allowing her husband (who spoke Mandarin) to carry on the conversation, but she obviously was enjoying the commotion of having her large and beautiful family home for the New Year holiday. Her house, which was Japanese in feel if not in actual architecture, stood across the street from a large Buddhist temple; her life seemed informed by its presence. That evening I sat in the little garden in back of the house drinking Johnny Walker Red with her second son and listening to the geckos cluck their tropical call. Lo Ch'ing's mother, whom I had met earlier that year, was very different. A robust and stately northerner, she spoke to me directly and in a Mandarin Chinese straight from Peking, buzzing with retroflexes and an occasional Pekingese ending. She was proud to provide the welcoming dinner for two jet-lagged friends of her oldest son. Her husband, a jovial and gentle man with a slight Hunan accent, held down the conversation before dinner (in halting English and measured Mandarin). But later, over watermelon, the room was hers as she smoked her Long Life cigarettes and watched the evening news. The lives and personalities of Yang Mu and Lo Ch'ing are radically different from those of their mothers, but the two poets have been influenced very much by the worlds their mothers represent.

Yang Mu 楊牧 (pen name for Wang Ching-hsien 王靖獻, b. 1940), and Lo Ch'ing 羅青 (pen name for Lo Ch'ing-che 羅青哲, b. 1948) both grew up on the island of Taiwan, which is the seat of power for the Chinese Nationalist Party, or Kuomintang (KMT), and its government, the Republic of China. But in family origins and relationship to the island Yang and Lo are very different. Yang's ancestors are native Chinese of the island, having resided there for several hundred years. Lo's family, on the other hand, came to Taiwan as part of the KMT retreat from the Communist victory on the mainland in 1949. While the story of the relationship between the Taiwanese natives and KMT-associated "mainlanders" is one tainted by violence and animosity, the lives of Yang and Lo are examples of the relatively successful integration of these two Chinese populations. (There is also an indigenous non-Chinese population on the island.) Yang has had a cordial relationship with the KMT government. Lo Ch'ing, who was born on the mainland, has become personally and professionally integrated into life in Taiwan, even though he has had many opportunities to make his home abroad.

Yang Mu's family comes from Hua-lien, a medium-sized town on the east coast that is known for its beautiful ocean and mountains, all punctuated by dramatic Toroko Gorge, which slices through the limestone and marble cliffs just outside the city (see his poem "Gazing Down"). As a Taiwanese family, they spoke both Taiwanese (at home) and Japanese (in official business) before the end of World War II. In many ways Yang grew up in a Japanese environment, speaking Japanese in the first years of his life and surrounded by it as he grew up. Some of his earliest memories are of the bombing and strafing attacks on his hometown by American planes during the war. By the time he entered public school, however, the Japanese rulers had been replaced by local Chinese ones and subsequently by the KMT (who tried to teach him to hate the Japanese and love the Americans) a few years later. After his somewhat tumultuous early years, Yang's middle childhood must have been relatively calm. His father, who ran a print shop, had the means to make sure his family, which expanded through the following years, lived in comfort.

Lo Ch'ing's childhood was much more straightforward and trauma-free. The turmoil of the war and his coming to Taiwan are not even a memory for him. By the time he was three his family had settled in Keelung, the port city for Taipei, where he grew up in relative comfort; his father worked in the shipping industry centered in that city. Lo Ch'ing did well in the school system administered by the KMT government; he was a model student with an early interest in painting. That interest brought him, at a young age, to the National Palace Museum, where he became a constant presence as he spent hours studying among the ancient ritual bronzes and Ming dynasty paintings.

Both Yang and Lo are oldest sons, which is a position of obvious prestige in their families. (Yang takes his actual surname,

Wang, from his mother's side; thus his next youngest brother, Yang Wei-chung, is the oldest son with his father's surname.) By any standards the two have fulfilled their filial roles well, bringing fame, if not always fortune, to the family. While all six of the Yang children are in academia and/or the art world, Yang Mu is certainly the one with the strongest international reputation. Neither of Lo Ch'ing's siblings is in academic work, although both are successful—his brother in the computer world of southern California and his sister in Taiwan as a television personality. The artistic reputations of Yang and Lo (Yang as a poet and essayist, Lo as a painter and poet) are widespread throughout China, especially in Taiwan but also in Hong Kong and recently to some extent on the mainland. Both are also well known as editors; Yang is a principal figure behind the very successful and prestigious Hung-fan publishing house, while Lo has been the editor of several literary journals and art books. Since the two poets also publish in the literary supplements of local newspapers (a relatively lucrative and exclusive vehicle), their names extend beyond literary circles. Moreover, Yang's reputation as a scholar (under the name C. H. Wang) is well established in Western sinological circles, while Lo Ch'ing's paintings have been collected and exhibited throughout Asia, the United States, and England.

Yang Mu's academic and professional career is a complicated and successful, if sometimes stormy, example of a Chinese person's accommodation to the West. By the time he graduated from Tung-hai University, a small private university known for its strong liberal arts program (where he was first a history, then an English, major), Yang was already an established poet in Taiwan, having won a national prize at the age of seventeen (writing under the pen name Yeh Shan). After a tour of duty in the army, he went to the Iowa Writers Workshop for a master of fine arts degree in the early 1960s, and then on to the University of California at Berkeley to study for a doctorate in comparative literature with Chen Shih-hsiang. Yang was one of the first Chinese of Taiwanese heritage to leave the island for an academic career in the United States. Under Chen's guidance Yang's interests in classical Chinese literature blossomed, such that his dissertation (and first scholarly book in English) used the Parry-Lord theory of oral formulaic poetry to analyze a Confucian classic, *The Book of Songs* (Shih ching). After a brief position at the University of Massachusetts, Amherst (where I first met him), Yang went to Seattle to teach at the University of

Washington, where he remains as a professor of Chinese and comparative literature. He travels often to Taiwan and elsewhere, but his home since 1971 has been Seattle. During that time, Yang has not only written a number of important academic articles in his professional field, he has also continued to write creatively. These works include volumes of poetry, essays, poetic drama, and memoirs, as well as several collections of prose and poetry that he has edited.

Lo Ch'ing's professional career runs somewhat parallel to Yang's, intersecting with it at one important juncture. Having attended some of the most prestigious public schools in the Keelung area, Lo graduated from Fu-jen University, a Catholic university in the Taipei suburbs, as an English major. In his junior year he began writing and publishing poetry, in addition to continuing his painting. Finding the cramped quarters of the college dormitory (six or eight students to a single room) too confining for painting, Lo began to do "verbal sketches" instead. After the requisite year in military service, Lo left for Seattle in 1972 to study for a master's degree in comparative literature with Yang Mu, with whom he had corresponded. Lo had already published quite widely by the time he left Taiwan, and his first book of poems, *Ways to Eat a Watermelon* (Ch'ih hsi-kua te fang-fa), was published and won a national prize the next year. In Lo's absence, his father accepted the award. In 1974 Lo left Seattle, returning to Taiwan after months of travel through the United States, Europe, and Asia. The focus on this "grand tour" was the art centers of the world, and his visits ranged from posing for a snapshot in front of Archibald MacLeish's house in Conway, Massachusetts, to visits to the Louvre. Upon his return to Taipei, Lo took a position teaching British and American literature at his alma mater, which he still holds along with a similar position at Taiwan Normal University. As the translations here attest, Lo continues a prolific career in poetry, but his writings also range from the academic article (in English as well as Chinese) to the lyrical essay. Most important is, however, his work as a painter, which has brought him national prestige and participation in international exhibitions.

The children of both poets have been important to their poetry. For Yang the birth of his son in 1980 was an event of profound significance, one that drew him even closer to his mother (his son carries her surname) and one that is celebrated repeatedly in his

14

poetry. Lo's two sons do not occupy such a personal presence in his poetry, but they are the examples closest at hand for his constant fascination with the "mind of the child." This interest has led Lo to compose and edit poetry for children, as well as to use their naive, disarming perspective in his own poems.

The relationship these two poets have with children is part of a larger approach to life, which in turn is reflected in their poetry. Yang's life is particularly intense and full of emotional response. There is a range of emotions, but they center on intimate friendship and romantic love. Yang has said that he does not find any pleasure in the abstract and theoretical, preferring to live a life fully engaged and charged with verve. He brings a profound intellect to reflect on his work and his life, and he commands a dynamic presence. Lo's personality is somewhat lower key, but is full of fun and goodwill. While on the surface Lo lives a rather conventional life, underneath there is a pervasive sense of the "trickster" in him, including a healthy sense of play and wit. Unlike Yang, Lo is fascinated with the theoretical and speculative. He is willing to entertain the latest idea, to allow room for the ephemerally modern, giving his life a constantly changing focus. This can lead to hectic movement from one project to the next, but Lo brings such energy to these given moments that there flows from them a sense of excitement and connection. While Yang's life is grounded in intellectual depth and personal strength, Lo's is one of wider breadth, informed by eclectic tastes. The poets bring these different personalities to their interactions with the outside world and to their art. In life and in art they are, each in his own way, dynamic, innovative, and of a generous spirit.

Two of the most recent times I saw Yang Mu and Lo Ch'ing they both were surrounded by their families. Yang, who had been dragged out of bed by his wife just to say hi to me (I had stopped by unannounced on my way to the airport), sat in his living room drinking tea, bundled in his robe and talking quietly, apparently nursing a hangover. The day before he had celebrated his forty-eighth birthday with his family, including his father, who was visiting from Taiwan: a day of sight-seeing, tennis, and eating. Yang's son, whom I also had not seen for years, was at his side, holding up the conversation in Mandarin and English with chat about his school and basketball playing. Yang looked on with deep pleasure.

After dinner at his mother's, Lo Ch'ing and I sat on his living room floor working the joy stick to a television video game in which a lollipop hero tries to negotiate a series of increasingly difficult passages. Lo was only slightly better at it than I was. His two sons kept flying back and forth from their bath to the living room, kibitzing and demonstrating how it was really done. Lo's wife laughed at the two of us, so comical and clumsy compared to those children of the 1980s.

FORBIDDEN GAMES
The Poetry of Yang Mu

From Taiwan to Iowa

From Ritual to Allegory

Risking the danger of endorsing excessive theorization of literature or, still worse, of tolerating the corruption of literary study currently evident in the games of critical jargon, I maintain that a proper approach in the comparative study of literature genetically unrelated is through the application of a tested theory. A tested theory is one that has been formulated first to assess an individual work in a particular tradition, used repeatedly on other works of similar nature and thereby revised and validated in that tradition. We apply it to the interpretation of works in another tradition. Often it is possible that, in so doing, we will illuminate these works with a strikingly new light and discover traits and messages never appreciated before. What we can find in literature of several traditions are not parallels or influences, but a common sense, a shared aspiration defined before individual backgrounds, an encyclopedia diversely cataloged, a poetry as a means of humanistic education. We fail if, instead of this, we fall back to piling more jargon upon jargon, confusing ourselves in the murky, infinitesimal units of the terminology popular in literary criticism but unknown in literature. For better or for worse, literary criticism is a key to literature. Literary criticism is not literature.

... Aware of the pitfalls scattered in various fashionable theories, I have chosen to adhere to what poetry itself has taught me, and to an organized set of literary concepts in the scholarly tradition. . . . If the poetry should appear to be inadequate as an expression of the progress of the Chinese humanities in that stage, I, not poetry, should be blamed. This book, written in English, seeks to identify the Chinese experiences of antiquity as the poets undertook to record their joys and sorrows in poetry, which, I believe, is immediate to our judgment when it is classified and subtitled according to the set of concepts. As much as I am eager to uncover the mysterious and the beautiful from a comparatist point of view, I am cautious to be obedient, as far as possible, to the great tradition of classical Chinese philology. I have tried to adjust our attitude toward affirming the position of some poems in a critical way, but I never wittingly invent anything to divest traditional philol-

From the preface, xiii–xiv.

ogy of its authority. We are removed from these poems by twenty-three to thirty centuries and, in the present case, by a greatly changed semantics under the impact of which I consider them, and further, by an entirely different language in which I manage to write about them. I hope that, in spite of all this, my efforts may still bring early Chinese poetry to a modern context to be appreciated by an audience unbelievable to its creators. Had it not been for this purpose, I would always write in Chinese.

消　　息

没有，在港上，用兩腳規
計算我的蒼白。

回家的路上，許多鳥屍，
許多睜圓了的而又笑著的眼。
執槍的人在茶肆裏擦汗，
看風景……

我們用雲做話題已是第九次了，
這傻子卻永遠美麗——
就是石板上的青苔也給坐死了，
煙囪也給數完了，
她依然愛笑，依然如此美麗！

一百零七次，用雲做話題，嗨！
她依然愛笑，依然美麗，
路上的鳥屍依然許多
執槍的人依然擦汗，在茶肆裏
看風景……

一九五八

The News

Over the bay, not plotting the dimensions of my pallor
With calipers.

The road home is strewn with the bodies of dead birds,
Their smiling eyes stare blankly.
In teahouses men armed with rifles wipe their sweaty brows,
Looking out at the scenery . . .

Nine times now we have talked of clouds,
This fool who is always so pretty—
The moss on the stone bench has succumbed to our sitting,
The smokestacks have all been counted,
And still she giggles, still so pretty.

And so, we have talked of clouds one hundred seven times,
And still she giggles, still so pretty,
The road is still strewn with dead birds.
Armed with rifles, men in teahouses still wipe their sweaty brows,
Looking out at the scenery . . .

1958

水之湄

我已在這兒坐了四個下午了
沒有人打這兒走過——別談足音了

（寂寞裏——）

鳳尾草從我袴下長到肩頭了
　　　不為甚麼地掩住我
說淙淙的水聲是一項難遣的記憶
我只能讓它寫在駐足的雲朵上了

南去二十公尺，一棵愛笑的蒲公英
風媒花把粉飄到我的斗笠上
我的斗笠能給你甚麼啊
我的臥姿之影能給你甚麼啊

四個下午的水聲比做四個下午的足音吧
倘若它們都是些急躁的少女
無止的爭執著
——那麼，誰也不能來，我只要個午寐
哪！誰也不能來

一九五八

The River's Edge

I have sat here these four endless afternoons

And no one has come—not even the tread of footsteps

(in silence)

The phoenix ferns have grown from thigh to shoulder

    Concealing me for no apparent reason

Claiming that the murmur of the river is a memory I can't shed

I can only let it be inscribed on the clouds that arrive

Twenty meters south dandelions smile

The wind sprinkles pollen on my peasant hat

But what can my hat offer you

What can my lounging shadow offer you

Perhaps the murmur of the river these four afternoons

Is a metaphor for the sound of footsteps these four afternoons

And both are the endless quarreling of nervous young girls

So no one can come, I need only to nap

No one can come

1958

風起的時候

風起的時候
廊下鈴鐺響著
小黃鸝鳥低飛簾起
你倚著欄杆，不再看花，不再看橋
看那西天薄暮的雲彩

風起的時候，我將記取
風起的時候，我凝視你草帽下美麗的驚懼
你肩上停著夕照
風沙咬嚙我南方人的雙唇

你在我波浪的胸懷
我們並立，看暮色自
彼此的肩膀輕輕地落下
輕輕地落下

一九六一・五

When the Wind Comes Up

When the wind comes up
The chimes under the colonnade ring
Orioles swoop low raising the curtain
You lean on the railing, no longer looking at the flowers,
    nor at the bridge
But at clouds pink in the western sunset

When the wind comes up, you will recollect how
When the wind came up I contemplated your sweet fear beneath
    the brim of your straw hat
The evening's light pausing on your shoulder
Wind-blown sand biting into my southerner's lips

You are in my thoughts crashing like the surf
As we stand side by side, watching the sun set
Lightly down our shoulders
Lightly down

May 1961

你住的小鎮

那兒的海灘像絲帶
細細地，白白地繞著
你住的小鎮像一面溜溜的鏡子
溜過風雲，溜過星月
卻繫住一百畝柔軟的陽光

陽光只為你一人的草帽
你住的小鎮，古老地
伸著手臂，在河岸上
在你的窗外描繪著一幢使館，一幢學院
在港口淺睡的小浪上
你走去，你是夕照

但這不是我的小鎮
當星光升上你的肩膀，你是黃昏
我悠閒泊船
「我家在山後
　那兒的海灘像絲帶」

一九六一‧十

The Town Where You Live

The beach there is like a ribbon of silk
Encircling, thin and white
The town where you live, a gleaming mirror
With the wind and clouds, stars and moon sliding by
But still tethered to acres of soft sunlight

And sunlight for your straw hat alone
The town where you live
Extends her arms anciently along the riverbank
Sketching an embassy, a college outside your window
On the ripples dozing in the bay
You leave, you are the evening light

But this is not the town where I live
When the star rises over your shoulder, you are the dusk
And I calmly bring my boat to its mooring
     "My home is on the other side of the mountains
     The beach there is like a ribbon of silk"

October 1961

微雨牧馬場

一排風蝕的斷水描出
異鄉的荒遼
有人倚靠柵欄
吹著柔柔的笛子
淺水穿流過你最愛的
芭蕉林，和閃爍的橋樑

雨季在我身上流出
巨石的紋路，眼看一群花斑馬
嘶鳴奔跑過微雨的一片
夢境的枯林——

倚著柵欄，我也腐朽了
變成一段牧馬場邊的枯木
只是潮濕了些
憂鬱了些

一九六三

A Ranch in the Rain

The dry reach of a wind-eroded stream describes

The wastes of a foreign land

Someone leans on the fence

Playing softly on a flute

And the shallow water flows through your favorite

Plantain farm and under the glittering bridge

Rain rolls off my body into

The striations of cliffs, a herd of horses

Runs through the dream's withered woods

Through the drizzle, neighing

Leaning on the fence, I too decay

Into a barren tree out near the ranch

But I am somewhat softer

Somewhat sadder

1963

在黑夜的玉米田裏

一

在黑夜的玉米田裏

枕著小河壩，夢見

春天的鷓鴣

從江岸上飛起來

像出岫的雲，黃昏

逐漸淡下去的酒旗，像悲哀

從造紙廠的煙囱曳長

照在銅架的鏡面上

「我的兩眼黯然，愛情和

戰時的燒夷彈一般」

焚去你一隻胳臂，一雙鞋，一本童話書

在黑夜的玉米田裏

你疲倦地枕著

微涼的小河壩，不停地思想

思想金蘋果樹枯槁的城，我們的城

飄雪的冬夜，飲酒的冬夜

有人為你編織毛襪

擦拭燭臺上的咖啡漬

蒼老的手勢

作別的歌

你的匕首，你的匕首

你的水囊，你的水囊

In the Cornfields of the Dark Night

1

In the cornfields of the dark night

Pillowing my head on the river dike, dreaming of

The spring partridge

Flying up from the riverbank

Like clouds rising above the mountains, dusk

And the fading tavern banner, like grief

Strung out from the smokestack of a paper mill

Shines in the bronze-framed mirror

"My eyes are gloomy, love is like

Napalm."

Burning away your arm, shoes, a book of nursery rhymes

In the cornfields of the dark night

Exhausted, you pillow your head

On the river dike, always thinking

Thinking about the town of withered apple trees, our town

In the winter night of snow flurries, the winter night of wine

Someone knits woolen socks for you

Wiping coffee stains off the candlestick

A decrepit gesture

A parting song

Your dagger and your canteen

Your dagger and your canteen

二

或是打烊以後的街道

旋轉的城堞

鐘響著

在遙遠的島上，鐘響著

你坐著讀信

並且傾聽馬達的聲音

井水

湧動你的影子

打碎了地下的星雲

「我的兩眼黯然，花掉在

夜夢的床上，我的兩眼……」

彷彿有許多春燈

許多放逐的雨夜

惦記著靠窗書架上的

杜萊登，*All for Love*

院子裏的足印，衣角，銅鈴

他是沒有歸途的雁，沒有歸途的

揚起又落下的灰塵

打開又關閉的窗

一九六五

2

Maybe on the street after the shops have closed

Near the spiraling, crenellated wall

A bell rings

On an island far away, a bell rings

As you sit reading my letter

Still listening to the motor

Water in the well

Rippling your reflection

Disintegrating the earthbound nebulas

"My eyes are gloomy, the flowers fall

On my bed of dreams, my eyes . . ."

As if there were springtime lamps aplenty

In the rainy nights of exile

Recalling how Dryden's *All for Love*

Lay on the bookcase near the window

The footprints in the yard, the edge of your skirt, the bronze bell

A wild goose with no way home, with no way home,

Raising up and letting fall the dust

Opening and closing the window

1965

四月二日與光中在密歇根同看殘雪

雨中繞過柏樹林，道路如
早春的河流。細小的礁石濺起
破碎的白浪，在卡拉瑪荣
一個圍著野煙的北方車站
純西洋的風景張貼在
死寂的庭院裏
　　　一列黑衣的修女

走到網球場邊，有人低聲說話——
過去我在水溝外看到一叢雛菊
我的大姐說：羅莎玲，羅莎玲，你回來
動身了，我們到湖邊去露營。他這樣說
他們端莊地沿著公寓牆外行走
如廢墟邊緣上的戰士

至於遠處，遠處只有紅磚的大樓
草場上埋葬去年的蟋蟀，去年的蟬
和知了聲裏紅裙的影子
砲聲驚起一城散步的灰鴿
宛若第一年的紅葉，玄學詩人的
　　　詭異：
　　　　　　鶩然，那人的柑橘園
　　　　　　橙黃的燈籠啊
　　　　　　掛在綠色的夜裏

April 2: With Yu Kwang-chung Watching the Michigan Snow Melt

In the rain, the road encircles the cypress woods like

A river in early spring. Waves break over

Sunken shoals, in Kalamazoo

A train station of the North, caught in a prairie fog

A purely Occidental landscape layered on

The deathly quiet courtyard

    A line of nuns dressed in black robes

Walking by the tennis court, someone says in a low voice—

Once beyond the canal I saw a clump of bluebells

My sister was calling, Rosalind, Rosalind, come back,

We are leaving, we are going to the lake camping. That's what she said

Stately they walk along the side of the apartment building

Like soldiers on the edges of a ruin

Over there a brick building stands tall and alone

Last year's crickets and cicadas are buried under the lawn

And the shadows of a red skirt caught in the katydid's song

The cannon blast startles the strutting doves, flying off

Like the red leaves of the first year, the strange images of

    The poet of exotica:

        Whose citrus orchard forthwith

        Hangs with orange lanterns

        In the green night

多少種水禽和雲朵深藏

在胸襟的一面湖泊上

安靜地汲水，乘著朔望佳日

没有速度的速度

月引灰濛濛的大地

環湖三州的節辰，驅散了復活的靈魂

　　那是誰拘謹的聲音？

　　　他說，羅莎玲，你不應該一個人

　　　　到蕎麥田去⋯⋯

　　　　　　　一九六六・十一・十

How many are the waterbirds and clouds that hide

The surface of the lake clinging to their breasts

They dip peacefully for water, taking advantage of the fine day

With speedless speed

The moon draws out the mist-shrouded world

A tristate Interlochen Festival, dispersing the reborn souls

    Whose voice is that, so tremulous?

        She says, Rosalind, you should not go all by yourself

        Out into those fields of wild wheat . . .

November 10, 1966

Berkeley and Beyond

From "The Weniad: A Chinese Epic in *Shih Ching*"

The five *Ta ya* poems in sequence . . . trace an epic experience of the early Chou [people] in search of a kingdom of heavenly justice. They sing of the mythical origin of the ancestor, the hardships posed before him, and how through great endurance he set up an eternal *figura* of cultural significance for ages to come. Accordingly, the poems tell how his offspring, highly conscious of their identity, wandered around, fought battles to defend their farms, houses, and temples, waiting for a supremely virtuous son to rise and define their heroism. King Wen was the *heros ktistes* who inherited the legacy of Lord Millet and momentously amplified it in accordance with the mandate of heaven. The mandate called for a change of government, through tyrannicide; it postulated a revolution in the classic sense. The poems also sing of the conquest led by King Wu in the final stage of the epic experience. This conquest signifies not the martial glory of the present leader but the magnanimity of the deceased hero, King Wen. The epic is the *Weniad* in spirit and action, to perpetuate the legacy of Lord Millet, according to this figural interpretation. King Wen, nevertheless, remains in the center of the interpretation, illuminating the true meaning of the *figura*. The relationships between him and Lord Millet and King Wu are, in the final analysis, ritualistic.

In function these poems approach liturgy. Individually examined, each appears to be in praise of one or more illustrious kings before the founding of the Chou dynasty. In this way, each poem serves to glorify the hero or heroes named or alluded to in the lines and stanzas. Moreover, it serves to warn the participants in the ritual, the living, against complacency and indolence which may rise in the wake of success. Collectively, the poems are comparable in this respect to the victory odes of Pindar and Bacchylides. The Greeks, like the Chou, realized that "insistent envy" always accompanied success. The reference to the endurance and humility of the ancestors as "small gourds," for instance, admonishes the inheritors of victory to guard against *hubris*. Bacchylides, in his fifth ode, reminds the Greeks both of the occasion of victory and

In *Essays in Commemoration of the Golden Jubilee of the Fung Ping Shan Library*, ed. Chan Ping-leung (Hong Kong: Hong Kong University Press, 1982), 141–42.

the suggestion of unhappiness: "Fearlessly make your heart cease from cares." The suggestion, in turn, corresponds to what Hsü Fu-kuan points out as the *yu-huan i-shih* of the Chou, a *sense* that adversity would never be entirely eliminated from life.

The *yu-huan i-shih* is thematic to the poems as a narrative sequence. It is on the basis of this understanding, by and large, that a class of poems has been selected from a large group to delineate and substantiate the *Weniad*. For these poems, while diverse in rhetorical forms, conform to the *sense*, which sustained the intense morality of the Chou in the first centuries of the dynasty. There are other poems in the *Ta ya* which similarly trace the splendid merits of the kings in the subsequent period, but they do not belong to the *Weniad*. It is not because they are different in form or language, nor because they do not mention King Wen; but because they fail to observe the legacy of Lord Millet as configured in King Wen—they have lost the *sense,* and are therefore unsuited to our interpretation in the context of the *Weniad*.

武宿夜組曲

　　1
一月戊午，師渡於孟津

　　2
只聽到雪原的鐘鼓
不停地喧噪，而我們
已經受了傷
樹也受了傷，爲征伐者取暖。惟有
征伐自身不惋惜待涉的河流
兵分七路

這正是新月遊落初雪天之際
我們傾聽赴陣的豐鎬戰士
那麼懦弱地哭泣
遺言分別繡在衣領上，終究還是
沒有名姓的死者——
孀寡棄婦蓺麻如之何？當春天
看到領兵者在宗廟裏祝祭
宣言一朝代在血泊裏
顫巍巍地不好意思地立起

King Wu's Encampment: A Suite of Songs

1

On the ides of January troops ford the river at Meng-chin

2

We hear only the drums on the snow-blown plains

Pounding ceaselessly, we

Have already been injured

And the trees have been injured too, providing warmth for the
   expedition

There is only the expedition itself, with no thought of the river

Crossing in seven lines of attack

When the crescent moon wanders the night of the first snows

We hear the troops from the towns of Chou move out in formation

Weeping softly so

On each collar embroidered their last will and testament, but in the end

They too are to be among the nameless dead—

Widows and abandoned wives so shall you reap. In spring

The commander offers his prayers in the ancestral hall

Declaring a new dynasty from the bloodbath arisen

Embarrassed and trembling

3

莫爲雄辯的睡意感到慚愧

慚愧疲勞在渡頭等你

等你沉默地上船蒼白地落水

落水爲西土定義一名全新的孀婦

孀婦

　　莫爲凱歸的隊伍釀酒織布

一九六九‧十一

3

No need to regret the drowsiness of elegant debates

Shame and fatigue await you at the river ford

Wait for you to board without a sound, then to plunge with ashen face

A plunge that defines the brand-new widows of the western land

Widows

    Prepare no robes no wine for the victors who come home this time

November 1969

續韓愈七言古詩「山石」

1

我與寺僧談佛畫，天明時
腳濕衣冷想的竟是城裏的
蜂群在梔子花間漫舞
竟是一婦人之坐臥
一幃幔之升降，或人
行走於筆硯經書的邊緣
談論玄武門之變
我對著月色，思維於
押韵險巇的漢魏詩；我的憤懣
是比主人的面容更虛無的

雖說我還須登衡山，謁楚神
面對豪雨刷亮的蕉林。所謂志向
滿佈泥濘如貶謫的南方
飲酒為蛇影所驚
歌唱赦書疾行

2

我與寺僧談佛畫，燈熄前
忽然憶及楊柳樹和
激激的流水也曾枕在耳際教我
浪漫如早歲的詩人一心學劍求仙
金釵羅裳和睡鞋就是愛情？

Continuing Han Yü's "Mountain Stones"

1

After the monk and I discuss the paintings on the temple wall, dawn comes

    dawn comes

With soaked feet and cold clothes I think of

The dance of bees among the gardenias in the city

Of a woman's chair and her bed

The rise and fall of a curtain, and someone

Walking on the edge of books and writing brushes

Discussing the coup at Hsüan-wu Gate

Facing the moonlight, my only thought is of

The oblique rhymes in the poetry of Han and Wei; my anger is

Emptier than the glances of my host

Although I still must climb Mount Heng to worship the goddess of Ch'u

I face the plantain leaves washed by heavy rains, my so-called ambition

As soggy as my southern exile

The shadows of serpents haunt the wine

Praises be sung; the amnesty is fleet of foot

2

After the monk and I discuss the wall paintings, the lamp not yet out

I suddenly recall how the willows

And swift waters on which I pillowed my head instructed me

To devote myself to swordsmanship and reclusion like the poet of the past

But is love merely in hairpins, slippers, and negligees?

我的學業是沼澤的腐臭和
宮庭的怔忡
我愛團扇
飛螢

但律詩寄內如無事件如鄜州
我只許渡江面對松櫪十圍
坐在酒樓上
等待流浪的彈箏人
並假裝不勝宿醉
我不該携帶三都兩京賦
卻愛極了司馬長卿

一九六八・一

My learning is the stench of the swamp

The anxiety of the court

Yet I love the fireflies

And the fan

The poem for my beloved is like Fu-chou, without incident

But I cross the river to look at the majestic pines

To sit upstairs in the wine shop

Pretending to be hung over

I wait for the wandering lute player

I should not have brought the "Urban Rhapsodies" with me

But I so love Ssu-ma Hsiang-ju

January 1968

將進酒四首

將進酒，乘太白。辦佳哉，詩審博。放故歌，心所作。同陰氣，詩悉索，使禹良工觀者苦。

——漢鏡歌第九

其一：逃逸之歌

而我們已經走出了火焰的圍城
這冷卻要讓你暈眩的血液
感到一種肯定。箭在嚴冬的
戰役裏被頑抗的守衛射出：
從烈火的垣堞向白雪

那一帶眨眼的河岸
莫非是埋怨慣了的港
我們赴敵前夕投宿的客棧
已經變成一棵含羞草，酒旗
搖不出破曉的天色
輕度失眠症使它無法忍受
任何放歸的船桅。從今以後

屠城的信號
與你無關

From "Bring on the Wine"

Bring on the wine, raise the ceremonial goblets
The debates will be wonderful, the poetry exact and expansive
Out with the old songs for what is in one's heart
Harmonizing with the dark side, the poetry will be done
And observers will know the toll of Yü's craft

Han Ritual Poem (9)

1. The Song of the Deserters

When we ran from the flames of the city where we lay siege

It was so cold your thinning blood

Might have sensed something positive in it. Deep in the winter war

Stalwart garrison troops shoot their arrows

Out from the blazing city walls into the snow

Isn't that blinking riverbank

The bay where complaints were often made

The inn where we spent our last night before the battle

Has been reduced to clumps of mimosa grass, the tavern's banner

Lies slack in the light of the breaking day

A minor case of insomnia prevents it from accepting

Any of the homeward sails. From now on

Signals from the burned-out city

Have nothing to do with you

其四：信天翁夜肆

坐在左邊的是猶太人。晚到的
祖籍波蘭據說是個演員
養了兩隻狼狗三隻貓和一個
很衰弱很秀麗的女人……

侍者無聲地端上一瓶冷卻的白酒
「二宮好江です！」

信天翁飛過舊詩的船桅
水蛇提醒你的罪。哲學刻在
木門上
左乾右坤上剝下復
　　　晚風在大街吹
急促的落花啊
　　　金笛玉簫喚不回

這踊子的腳步是極細碎的
滿室游走又若風在水面
拂過了沉船的漩渦
又舞成一片臨江的新葉
射落的信天翁不帶一滴血
投影在水曜日的約會

　　　　　　　　　　　一九六九・九

4. A Night at the Albatross

On my right sits a Jew of Polish extraction

Arriving late he is said to be an actor

Raising two German shepherds, three cats, and a

Woman, lovely and delicate . . .

And a waitress brings rice wine on a tray, its warmth already lost

"Ninomiya Yoshie desu," she says, introducing herself

An albatross flies over the sails of ancient verse

The water snake awakens your sin. Philosophy carves magic hexagrams

On the wooden door

"Heaven" to the left, "Earth" to the right, "Depart" above,

    "Return" below

    In the avenue the evening wind blows

The hastily falling flowers down

    Neither golden flute nor jade oboe can call them home again

The steps of the *odoriko* dancer are so dainty

Her swirling fills the room like wind

Brushing over the whirlpool left by a sinking ship

Her dance mutates into spring leaves on the riverbank

And shot, the albatross falls bloodlessly dead

Casting its shadow over our appointment on *suiyobi* day

September 1969

猝不及防的花

一朵猝不及防的花
如歌地淒苦地
生長在黑暗的滂沱：
而歲月的葬禮也終於結束了
以蝙蝠的翼，輪迴一般
遮蓋了秋林最後一場火災

弔亡的行列
自霜
和汽笛中消滅
一顆垂亡的星
在南天臨海處嘶叫

而終於也有些骨灰
這一捧送給寺院給他給佛給井給菩提
眼淚永生等等抽象的，給黃昏的鼓
其餘的猶疑用來榮養一朵猝不及防的花

一九七〇

Surprise Lilies

Surprise lilies

Songlike and sorrowful

Growing in the torrential darkness:

And the burial service for the months and years has finally concluded

With the wings of the bat cyclically

Smothering the last fire in the autumnal forest

The funeral procession

Vanishes into the frost

And foghorn

A dying star moans

Above the ocean in the southern sky

And in the end there are funerary ashes

A handful, for the monastery, for him, for Buddha, for the well,

    for nirvana

Tears, eternity, and such abstractions, and for the drums of sunset

The doubt that remains is sustenance for the lilies

1970

風在雪林裏追趕

風在雪林裏追趕
以車輪的姿勢,快樂地
互相戲謔著,褪色的喧囂
最遠處是不曾霽過的
一棵山毛櫸,然則風
在雪林裏追趕

以繁星破碎的聲音
以奔流的氣味,以瓜果的
膨脹——風在雪林裏
為嶄新的疲憊佈置一則
彈乎冉殼般結實而空洞的預言
已經是倒塌了的骨骼,所以

風在雪林裏追趕
越過一片片衰弱的陽光
零亂的欲望,下陷的牀
和昨晚最最黑暗的水柳;越過
昨晚最黑暗的水柳,果然風
在雪林裏追趕

一九七一·三·九

The Wind Rolls
through the Snowy Woods

The wind rolls through the snowy woods

With the bearing of an automobile, gaily

It cavorts with itself, fading chatter

Farthest away are beech trees where snow still lingers

And hence the wind

Rolls through the snowy woods

With the sound of shattering stars,

The smell of cascades, with the fullness of

Fruit—the wind in the snowy woods

Arranges for a lethargy new and improved

Predictions as empty and hard as spent rounds of ammunition

The skeletons have already collapsed, therefore

The wind rolls through the snowy woods

Passing over the decaying sunlight

The fragmented wishes, the sunken bed

And last night's darkest willow; it passes over

Last night's darkest willow, and, as expected, the wind

Rolls through the snowy woods

March 9, 1971

夏　天

一些烟
很多很多的綠
盤旋的蚊蟲，晚香玉
馬克東納先生抽烟斗
修籬笆。好一片片飛落的榆錢

隔著浮滿綠苔的池塘

因爲樹林子太深了
就顯得啄木鳥的努力是
預報黃昏雨的鼓點
除了這個，四畝方圓
幾乎都是病了破碎的天

一九七一・六・六

Summertime

Wisp of smoke

Green, green

Mosquitoes circle, lilies white

McDonald smokes his pipe

Fixing the fence. One by one elm leaves flutter down

Near the pond where green algae grows

The woods are so deep

That the work of the woodpecker sounds like

A drum roll announcing the arrival of the evening rain

Except for this, a four-acre lot

Almost everything is sick and shattered light

June 6, 1971

十四行詩十四首

一

四月是一片纏綿迎拒的
園子，衣裳上的刺繡
猶如覷覰的五代
牡丹芍藥卻已經是
一卷漸漸豪放的宋詞了

鬢髮印著
短欄杆的丁香色澤——
一些水玉羅襪交錯在十指緊抓的
痕跡。惱人的更漏子
支頤的委頓，久久地無言
雙眉如寒禽撲翅
眼是微閉的五更星：
還能看見地上初生的薄荷罷
踏斷的香味揉在風裏

二

血脈裏積著濃霧
一炮輪凌晨快行
企圖闖關。這種事件
年年晚春總是發生的

From "A Set of Fourteen Sonnets"

1

April is a garden intertwined and
Undecided, the embroidered blouse
As bashful as the Five Dynasties
But peony and paeonia are already
A scroll of Sung poetry with its increasing bravura

Imprinted on her temples
The fragrance of the balustrade lilac—
The seizing marks of crystalline stockings interlacing
her toes. The clepsydra that drives men mad
Head in hands, weary, so long without a word
Eyebrows flutter like the wings of birds against the cold
Eyes are the stars of early dawn nearly closed
But can't you see the mint growing again
Its trampled fragrance rolling in the wind

2

As the thick fog collects in my veins
The gunship of early morn speeds on its way
Intending to breach the pass. This is a thing
That happens almost every spring

惡徒多數向我繳械
投降——這時月落星沉
黃鶯在枝上啼
溫存的彩色在荷葉的
正綠裏滾動變化
黑髮如北寒帶
在記憶中澎湃
群馬奔過幽暗的
草原，細雨飄落
你黃梅樹的窗前

一九七三

Enemy troops surrender en masse

Submitting to me—when the moon descends, stars fade

And in the branches orioles sing

The color of warm air seeps through the essential green

Of lotus leaves and transforms them

Black hair like the arctic circle

Undulating in my memory

Horses gallop across the dark

Plain, a fine rain floats down

On the summer plum in your window

1973

鷓鴣天六首

一　常綠喬木

草地並不很濕
星星佈滿池塘
我們還不曾迷路
花香不像是從地上來的
輕輕地，彷彿
從你兩肩——

在我雙手合攏處
有一片漸晚的雲
低溫的氣流飄過
陰森森的常綠喬木

二　衣袖

我們開始飲酒
當暗夜充滿
四段互相取暖的衣袖：
我們是徬徨的梧桐樹

開始訴說風雪的聲
和無聲。冬天裏總聽著
同一張不記得標題的唱片
枯槁的枝枒撐起
蕭索臨窗一夢

Six Songs to the Tune ''Partridge Skies''

1. Douglas Fir

The lawn is not really very damp

Stars fill the small pool

And we have not yet lost our way

As if the flower's fragrance rose not from the ground

But delicately

From your shoulders—

Where my two hands interlace

A cloud moves into the evening

Warm air seeps over

The gloomy firs

2. Sleeves

We begin to drink

When the dark night is full upon us

Our four sleeves cuddle together for warmth:

We are hesitating catalpa trees

Starting to complain of the noise and silence

Of wind-blown snow. In the winter we are always listening

To the same record, I forget the title

The withered branches lift up

A chilling dream past the window

「我是懂得愛的」
我們開始飲酒：「而且
一直在期待著愛的發生」

三　水鳥

一如舟楫停止在無風的湖心
我們停止在雨舷之間一片雲
雖然無風，卻隨著你的微息
爲舟楫停止無風湖心之飄搖

好多年代都過去了，愛的
年代——船底積滿
青苔和貝殼
在那無風的湖心
你猶未完全憔悴
猶是瘦削地羞紅
如夕陽下的水鳥

四　我的女蘿

你也曾經散髮解衣
向著菊花怒放的廢墟
而我仰望衆神
如何踴躍地死滅
旋轉，纏綿

"I know about love"

(We begin to drink)

"And I am always waiting for it to come"

3. Swan

Like a boat adrift in the middle of a windless lake

We float on this white cloud between the gunwales

No wind, but with your light breathing

We rock like a boat adrift in the middle of a windless lake

The ages have slipped by, ages of

Love—the bottom of the boat is covered

With moss and barnacles

In the middle of that windless lake

You have not yet lost your bloom

You are still delicate and pink

Like a swan in the sunset

4. My Loving Vine

Letting down your hair, taking off your clothes

You face the ruins abloom with chrysanthemums

And I gaze up at the host of gods

Joyfully perishing

Swirling, intertwining

成為我的衛星
我的女蘿

那時你就了解
我是多麼荒涼
遙遠，你又是
多麼地輕微
零落

五　菊花

那時你就應該
了解愛是紅柿子
和薄荷香混雜在
一兩册詩集裏的
氣味。你也無須再
扭動兩肩說要延期

你不如就把一切絲織品
取下，留著項鍊和耳墜
當車輛輾過積水的巷子
聲音更遠更小的時候
當座鐘開始抖動我們的
時間，菊花合蒂落在枕上
並且散開的時候
你也不如散開

Becoming my satellite

My loving vine

Then you understood

How desolate and distant

I was and how light and spare

You were

My loving vine

5. Chrysanthemums

You should have understood then

That love is in the aroma of mint and

Ripe persimmons mixed with

Books of poetry. There was

No need for you

To turn your back and say we should wait

You might as well shed your silk garments

Leaving on your necklace and earrings

When the sound of tires rolling through the flooded alley

Becomes distant and faint

When the grandfather clock shakes our

Time, and the chrysanthemums fall on the pillow

Petals spreading out across the bed

You might as well do the same

六　河岸

這樣散開很好
零落的琴聲
眼睛是頹廢派的
燈籠，寒毛是十字軍
露宿的草原

殘雲在四肢
星升到了額頭
月浸在水裏
腹下是一朵碩大的花
簷滴的聲音
和形象，抽搐的血脈
和崩潰的骨骼

又有一片更溫暖的河岸
看到我們畏懼地坐著
依靠著

一九七四‧一

6. Riverbank

Spreading out like that is so nice

Lute music drifting in

Your eyes are the lamps of the

Decadent School, your hair the grassy plains

Where crusaders stay the night

Scattered clouds surround your limbs

Stars rise to shine on your forehead

The moon slides into the river

Below your belly is a blossom spreading

The sound of rain falling off the eaves

And its image, fluttering veins

And scattered skeletons

And an even warmer riverbank

Watches us sit anxiously

Clinging to each other

January 1974

秋祭杜甫

我並不警覺，惟樹林外
隱隱滿地是江湖，嗚呼杜公
當劍南邛南罷兵窺伺
公至夔州，居有頃
遷赤甲，瀼西，東屯
還瀼西，歸夔。這是如何如何
飄蕩的生涯。一千二百年以前……
觀公孫大娘弟子舞劍器
放船出峽，下荊楚
嗚呼杜公，竟以寓卒

如今我廢然望江湖，惟樹林外
稍知秋已深，雨雲聚散
想公之車迹船痕，一千二百年
以前的江陵，公安，岳州，漢陽
秋歸不果，避亂耒陽
尋靈均之舊鄉，嗚呼杜公
詩人合當老死於斯，暴卒於斯
我如今仍以牛肉白酒置西向的
窗口，並朗誦一首新詩
嗚呼杜公，哀哉尚饗

一九七四

An Autumnal Prayer to Tu Fu

I did not realize that beyond the woods

Lurked a wild world

South of Chien and Ch'iung, troops lying in wait

You went out to K'uei-fu for a visit

Then on to Ch'ih-chia, Jang-hsi, Tung-t'un

Back to Jang-hsi, and home again to K'uei-fu. And thus you went

Drifting through the borders of your life. 1,200 years ago . . .

Then "seeing Madam Kung-sun's young student perform the sword
    dance"

You sailed down through the gorges to Ching and Ch'u

Dying en route

Exhausted I now gaze upon that wild world beyond the woods

Knowing that autumn is upon us, clouds and rain gather and scatter

Thinking of the traces of your travel, 1,200 years ago

Chiang-ling, Kung-an, Yüeh City, and Han-yang

The autumn homecoming was never to be, fleeing trouble in Lei-yang

Seeking the old home of Ch'ü Yüan

All poets should grow old and die there, or die young there

Again I offer you beef and pure wine in the window facing

West, and sing to you this new song

Praying that you accept my gift

1974

Taiwan Again

From "The Bird as Messenger of Love in Allegorical Poetry"

Instead of the turtledove, Ch'ü Yüan sends the snake-falcon as a messenger of love. The choice is a tragic one, because the snake-falcon is inept for such a mission. It can never be received with grace by society. When the snake-falcon returns and tells that the suit is amiss, it actually says that the lady in the tower refuses to accept its entreatment. The snake-falcon, obviously a *persona non grata*, may not even have the chance to present the case to the lady. There is, however, always something upright in *persona non grata;* and, in choosing the snake-falcon and rejecting the turtle-dove, Ch'ü Yüan shows his appreciation of the quality of upright-ness—over slyness—in his messenger. For the messenger of love ought to be compatible with its master in heart and mind. The bad reputation of the snake-falcon is probably due to slander, too, as that of Ch'ü Yüan definitely is.

Between the slandered and the sly birds, Ch'ü Yüan chooses the former, the non-conformist, because he himself, though not literally "poisonous," is as mistreated as the bird is by society. He realizes that he is "alone at a loss" in the world where everything has turned upside down, and once he even compares himself to the eagle:

Eagles do not flock like other birds—
So it has been true since antiquity.

The snake-falcon resembles the eagle in certain respects; for in-stance, it does not seek to flock with others like the lesser birds. Ch'ü Yüan uses it for its independent spirit, despite its bad reputa-tion. The choice, therefore, reveals a certain degree of pathetic fal-lacy on the part of the frustrated courtier. Perhaps out of protest, he identifies himself with the snake-falcon, the bird which is much slandered for its refusal to please the self-deceiving majority in a chaotic age. Ch'ü Yüan has been deprived of his title, but he does not believe it is appropriate to regain it at the cost of honor and justice. There is at the same time despair and pride in his search of

New Asia Academic Bulletin 1 (1978): 75–76.

truth throughout *Li sao*. His determination not to compromise with the wicked but to attack them, therefore, elevates him to a point where he is both high and lonely. Still, he refuses to succumb to ignorance, though he can succumb to death.

情　詩

金橘是常綠灌木
夏日開花，其色白其瓣五
長江以南產之，屬於
芸香科

屬於芸香科眞好
花椒也是，還有山枇杷
黃檗，佛手，檸檬
還有你

你們這一科眞好
（坐在燈前吃金橘）
名字也好聽，譬如
九里香，全株可以藥用

受命不遷生南國兮
故事也好聽（坐在
燈前吃金橘）后皇嘉樹
以喻屈原

你問我屬於甚麼科
大概是楝科吧
臺灣米仔蘭，是
常綠喬木的一種，又叫

A Love Poem

The kumquat is a nondeciduous shrub
Flowering in the summer, with a white blossom of five petals
It grows south of the Yangtze, belonging to the
Rutaceae family, genus *Fortunella*

Belonging to the Rutaceae family is fine indeed
So do the flowering pepper and the loquat
The philodendron, the bergamot, the lemon
And you

This family of yours is really very fine
(Eating kumquats in the light of the lamp)
The names are pleasing to the ear, for example
The Plant of Pervading Fragrance—the whole tree has medicinal uses

"As he commanded, it stays, growing in the Southern Land"
This is also pleasing (eating kumquats
In the light of the lamp) "Fairest of all God's trees"
As an emblem of Ch'ü Yüan

You ask about me
Probably I belong to the Melia family
An *Aglaia odorata* of Taiwan
A tall evergreen, that is also called

紅柴，土土的名字
樹皮剝落不好看
生長沿海雜木林中
也並沒有好聽的故事

木質還可以，供支柱
作船舵，也常用來作
木錘。憑良心講
眞是土

一九七四‧十二

The redbark, such a common name,

Its peeling bark unsightly

Grows in mixed forests along the sea

But has no pleasing story of its own

The wood is all right, it's good for pillars

They make rudders from it, and it is often used for

Mallets. Actually

It is really quite common

December 1974

高雄・一九七三

這條船的形式完全爲内容所決定，港的顏色爲旗山，風的方向爲情感，心的志忐爲一種經緯度的轉換——所決定，想著這些，站在加工出口區照像，忽然忽然看到細雨從四處飄來聚合，羞辱的感覺比疲倦還明快，切過有病的胸膛。

資深的港務員有禮地追憶他初到時，這港的顏色如何爲戰爭，形式如何爲旗山，潮水如何爲風所決定。他的口音證明他是閩侯世家的游子，話裏夾插英文術語。這麽好的教養，在上一代的港務員當中據說是不多見的。「上海因黃浦江的泥沙而淤淺了，」他說：「正如鹿港。」「没落了，」他說：「所以高雄是中國第一大商港。」

午後的高雄開始蒸發沉重的濕度，這條船的形式逐漸解體，廢油漂在水面上，暫時的晴朗，又把貨櫃碼頭晒乾。我們沿著鐵道走，不時站好，照像。資深的港務員仍然有禮地爲我們說明貨櫃裝載作業的程序，話裏夾插英文術語。忽然一場大雨，三萬五千各女工同時下班，而我的羞辱的感覺比疲倦還明快，切過有病的胸膛。

八月

Kaohsiung, 1973

The shape of the ship is dictated completely by its cargo, the color of the harbor by Banner Mountain, the direction of the wind by emotion, the heart's queasiness by a change in coordinates—everything dictated so; pondering this we stand taking snapshots in the Export Processing Zone, suddenly, quite suddenly a light rain sweeps in from all directions gathering there, and a feeling of shame sharper than fatigue cuts through my sick heart.

Politely the well-trained harbor employee recalls how, when he first came here, the color of the harbor was dictated by war, the shape by Banner Mountain, the tides by the wind. His accent attests to his Fukienese heritage, but he keeps inserting English terms into his talk. Such an education as this, I hear, would have been rare among the harbor employees of the previous generation. "Because of the silting of the Huangpu River, the harbor at Shanghai has become shallow," he says, "just like Lu-kang." "It's washed up," he says, "therefore Kaohsiung is now China's largest harbor."

Kaohsiung begins to cook under the pressure-cooker heat of the late afternoon, the shape of the ship slowly disintegrates, waste oil floats on the surface of the water, the sky clears, and the container dock is baked dry. We walk along the railroad tracks, stopping

often to take snapshots. The well-trained harbor employee goes on politely explaining the procedure for filling and loading the containers, inserting English terms into his talk. Suddenly there is a rainstorm; thirty-five thousand women pour out of the buildings; a feeling of shame sharper than fatigue cuts through my sick heart.

August

你的心情

一

你的心情我想我知道
當黃昏自聖誕紅上褪色
黑夜在屋頂上，黑夜在
紅瓦暗淡的屋頂上梭巡
啊你的心情好像那霜雪
我試探著，感覺七尋下的
微溫，那裏曾經有一座火山
火山是你的心情我知道

二

你的心情我想我知道
當黑夜自夾竹桃上消逝
霜雪在我兩鬢，霜雪在
我風雨絕迹的兩鬢停留
啊你的心情好像那冰崖
我尋覓著，聽到萬年以前的
布穀，那裏曾經有一片草原
草原是你的心情我知道

三

你的心情我想我知道
當白日以蘆葦花爲你
織好一條溫暖的圍巾

What Is in Your Heart

1

I think I know what is in your heart

As sunset fades on the poinsettia leaves

Night is on the roof wandering to and fro

On the vaguely darkened, red-tiled roof

Your heart is like frost and snow

But I probe, feeling the warmth seven fathoms

Below, where once there was a volcano

It's a volcano that is in your heart, this I know

2

I think I know what is in your heart

As the dark night vanishes on the oleander

Frost and snow linger

On my brow without a trace of wind or rain

Your heart is like an icy ledge

But I search, hearing the cuckoo of a million years

Ago where once there were grasslands

Grasslands are in your heart, this I know

3

I think I know what is in your heart

As the day weaves for you a scarf

Out of white rushes

一頂帽子，一襲臨風的衣裳
啊你的心情好像那雲霧
我摸索著，看見浩瀚的
波浪，那裏曾經有一片海洋
海洋是你的心情我知道

　　　　　　　　　　　　　一九七六・一

A hat, a suit of clothes in the wind

Your heart is like the mist and clouds

But I grope, seeing gigantic

Waves where there once was a sea

A sea is in your heart, this I know

January 1976

蘆葦地帶

一

那是一個寒冷的上午
在離開城市不遠的
蘆葦地帶，我站在風中
想像你正穿過人群——
竟感覺我十分歡喜
這種等待，然而我對自己說
這次風中的等待將是風中
最後的等待

我數著陽臺裏外的
盆景，揣測榕樹的年代
看清晨的陽光斜打
一朵冬天的臺灣菊
那時你正在穿過人群
空氣中擁擠著
發光的焦慮
我想阻止你或是
催促你，但我看不見你

我坐下摩挲一把茶壺
觸及髹漆精緻的彩鳳雙飛翼
和那寓言背後的溫暖
滿足於我這個年紀的安祥

A Stand of Reeds

1

A chilly morning

In a stand of reeds

Not far from the city, in the wind I stand

Imagining that you are just now making your way through the crowds—

I realize I am infatuated

With this waiting, and say to myself

This wait in the wind will be

The last wait in the wind

Counting the bonsai plants beyond the

Balcony, speculating on the age of the banyan tree

I watch the morning sunlight skitter across

The pot of Taiwanese chrysanthemums

You are now just making your way through the crowds

In the air there is such a crush of

Bright brooding

I want to stop you or to

Urge you on, but I cannot see you

I sit here fondling the wings

Of nuptial phoenixes and the warmth of their parable

Caught in the ruby glaze of the teapot

Contented with the serenity of my age

我發覺門鈴的意像曾經
出現在浪漫時期，印在書上
已經考過的那一章
我翻閱最後那幾頁
唯心的結構主義，懷疑
我的推理方式是不是
適合你，袛知道我不能
強制你接受我主觀的結論
決心讓你表達你自己

二

決心讓你表達你自己
選擇你的判斷，我不再
追究你如何判斷
你的選擇，歲月
是河流，忽陰忽陽
岸上的人不能追究
閃爍的得失

甚至我必須
向你學習針黹
一邊鈎毛線一邊說話
很好很閑適的神色
袛是笑容流露出
些許不寧，有時
針頭扎疼了纏著線團的
食指：是的你也和我一樣

I discover that the image of the doorbell has already

Been used in romances, and what is printed in the book

Is an essay that has already received a passing grade

I skim through the last few pages of

This theoretical method, wondering if

My speculations are in any way

Appropriate to you, knowing only that I cannot

Force you to accept my conclusions

But must allow you to express yourself

2

I must allow you to express yourself

To make your own judgments, I will not again

Probe how you judge

How you choose as you do, time is

A river, yin and yang, dark and light

Someone on the bank cannot probe

The gain and loss of all that glitter

I must

Study the way you knit

Stitching as you talk

So refined and relaxed

Only your laugh betrays

The trouble, occasionally

The needle pricks your finger

Wound in coils of yarn: you and I are alike

強自鎮靜的，難免還是
難免分心

那是一個寒冷的上午
我們假裝快樂，傳遞著
微熱的茶杯。我假裝
不知道茶涼的時候
正是彩鳳冷卻的時候
假裝那悲哀是未來的世界
不是現在此刻，雖然
日頭越升越高，在離開
城市不遠的蘆葦地帶
我們對彼此承諾著
不著邊際的夢
在比較廣大的快樂的
世界，在未來的
遙遠的世界

直到我在你的哭聲中
聽到你如何表達了你自己
我知道這不是最後的
等待，因爲我愛你

一九七七・一

Forcing ourselves to be composed, but it is impossible

Not to be distracted

A chilly morning

We pretend to be happy, passing the cups

of tepid tea. I pretend

Not to notice it has gone cold

As the phoenixes have also cooled

Pretending that grief belongs to a time yet to come

Not now, although at this moment

The sun climbs higher and higher, in the

Stand of reeds not far from the city

We make promises

Of empty dreams

In times of greater joy

In times far off

Yet to come

When I hear how you express yourself

In tears

I know then that this isn't the last time

I'll wait, because I love you

January 1977

孤　　獨

孤獨是一匹衰老的獸
潛伏在我亂石磊磊的心裏
背上有一種善變的花紋
那是，我知道，他族類的保護色
他的眼神蕭索，經常凝視
遙遙的行雲，嚮往
天上的舒卷和飄流
低頭沈思，讓風雨隨意鞭打
他委棄的暴猛
他風化的愛

孤獨是一匹衰老的獸
潛伏在我亂石磊磊的心裏
雷鳴刹那，他緩緩挪動
費力地走進我斟酌的酒杯
且用他戀慕的眸子
憂戚地瞪著一黃昏的飲者
這時，我知道，他正懊悔著
不該冒然離開他熟悉的世界
進入這冷酒之中，我舉杯就唇
慈祥地把他送回心裏

一九七六・三

Solitude

Solitude, that decrepit beast

Crouches in my stone-strewn heart

Its back patterned with colors of easy change

Meaning, I know, he is of chameleon genes

The glint of his eye is hard, always fixed

On the distant rolling clouds, aspiring to

The sky's flight and flow, its spread and roll

Head lowered in thought, he lets the wind whip as it would

His abandoned violence

His eroded love

Solitude, that decrepit beast

Crouches in my stone-strewn heart

At the instant of the thunder clap, he slowly turns

Making his way into my glass of rum

And with eyes of admiration and love

Stares sadly at the evening drinker

This time surely regretting

How hastily he abandoned his world

For this one of chilling rum, I raise the glass to my mouth

And kindly send him back home again

March 1976

水田地帶

下一個春天和下下一個春天
我站在微雲灌滿活水的田裏，想像
你是美麗的鷺鷥
潔白的衣裳
脆弱的心

而現在我們坐在田埂上
背後有人在順風焚燒一些稻桿
青煙吹在我們兩個人中間

下一個夏天和下下一個夏天
我可能再來看稻穗吹南風的海浪
看蜻蜓遮蔽半片藍色的天
你在另外一個國度
也許永遠不回來了

而現在我們沿著公路走
發現田裏不開花的是水仙
我們大笑，淡水河橫在左手邊

下一個秋天和下下一個秋天
我決心為他們扮演沉默的稻草人
可是我答應你了我絕對不嚇你

A Stand of Rice

Next spring, or the spring after
I will stand in the flooded paddy with wisps of clouds overhead,
Imagining you are an egret elegantly
Clothed in pristine white
And a delicate heart

But now we sit on the paddy dike
Downwind from someone burning rice straw
Its blue smoke blows between us

Next summer, or the summer after
Perhaps I will come again to watch the waves of rice blowing
    through the southern wind
To watch the blue sky obscured by clouds of dragonflies
But you will be in another country
Maybe never to return

But now walking along the highway
We discover the flowers bent over the pool are indeed narcissus
And we laugh, the Tamsui River is on our left

Next fall, or the fall after
I will be their silent scarecrow
But I will not scare you

就有那麼幾個秋天
我這樣枯等著

而現在我們並立候車
交換著幾個月來聽到的故事
錯以為我們可以這樣把距離拉近

下一個冬天和下下一個冬天——
其實我已經覺悟再也不會有
下一個冬天。他們在焚燒著
沉默盡職的稻草人
青煙在樹林子外盤旋

而現在我們在前往的船上
前往永遠不再的水田地帶
為了證明這是幻想不是愛

一九七七·二

There are only a few falls left

In which I will dumbly wait

But now we stand side by side waiting for the bus

Exchanging stories of the past few months

Deceiving ourselves into believing we can reach across that distance

Next winter, or the winter after—

But actually I already know that there won't be

A next winter. They are burning the

Silent, vigilant scarecrow

The blue smoke swirling out beyond the woods

But now we are on a boat going off

Off toward a stand of rice that will never be again

In order to prove this is an illusion, not love

February 1977

熱蘭遮城

一

對方已經進入燠熱的蟬聲
自石級下仰視，危危潤葉樹
張開便是風的床褥——
巨砲生銹。而我不知如何於
硝煙疾走的歷史中冷靜踟躕
她那一襲藍花的新衣服

有一份燦然極令我欣喜
若歐洲的長劍斗膽挑破
顚倒的胸襟。我們拾級而上
鼓在軍中響，而當我
解開她那一排十二隻紐扣時
我發覺迎人的仍是熟悉
涼爽的乳房印證一顆痣
敵船在海面整隊
我們流汗避雨

二

敵船在積極預備拂曉的攻擊
我們流汗佈署防禦
兩隻枕頭築成一座砲臺
蟬聲漸漸消滅，亞熱帶的風
鼓盪成波動的床褥

Zeelandia

1

The place across the way has sunk into the burning chirr of the cicada

Looking up from the stone steps, the soaring tree

Spreads its broad leaves, a mattress for the wind—

The huge cannon is rusting. But I wonder how

To trample heartlessly upon her new blue dress

In the history of frantic gunfire

There is a sadness that brings me great pleasure

Like the European swords boldly slicing open

Inverted necklines. I mount the stairs

With the roll of battle drums, and I unbutton

The dozen buttons on her blue dress

To discover the one who welcomes me is the familiar

Cool breast attesting to the mole

The enemy ships are arrayed along the shore

We sweat to get out of the rain

2

At daybreak the enemy ships are poised for an attack

We sweat arranging our fortress

Two pillows for a cannon mount

The call of the cicada slowly fades, tropical winds

Pound into the mattress of rolling waves

你本是來自他鄉的水獸
如此光滑如此潔淨
你的四肢比我們修長

你的口音彷彿也是清脆的
是女牆崩落時求救的呼喊
彷彿也是枯井的虛假
我俯身時總聽到你
空洞的回聲不斷

三

巨砲生銹，硝煙在
歷史的斷簡裏飛逝
而我撫弄你的腰身苦惱
這一排綠油油的濶葉樹又在
等候我躺下慢慢命名

自塔樓的位置視之
那是你傾斜的項鍊一串
每顆珍珠是一次戰鬥
樹上佈滿火拼的槍眼

動人的荷蘭在我硝煙的
懷抱裏滾動如風車

You are actually a waterbeast from abroad

Glistening and pristine

Your limbs are more slender than ours

Your accent crystalline

A scream for help under crumbling ramparts

Also seems as empty as a dry well

When I lie listening to your

Vacant endless echoes

3

The huge cannon is rusting, the gunfire

Flies through the fragmented pages of history

And I caress your waist worry

About the row of glistening green, broadleaf trees

That wait for me to slowly name them again from below

Looking from the tower

Your necklace hangs aslant

Each jewel a battle

And the trees are arrayed with bullet holes

Beautiful Holland moves like a windmill

In my gunfire embrace

四

默默數著慢慢解開
那一襲新衣的十二隻紐扣
在熱蘭遮城，姐妹共穿
夏天易落的衣裳：風從海峽來
並且撩撥著掀開的蝴蝶領
我想發現的是一組香料群島啊，誰知
迎面升起的仍然只是嗜血的有著
一種薄荷氣味的乳房。伊拉
福爾摩莎，我來了仰臥在
你涼快的風的床褥上。伊拉
福爾摩莎，我自遠方來殖民
但我已屈服。伊拉
福爾摩莎。伊拉
福爾摩莎

一九七五‧一

4

Silently counting the slowly unbuttoned

Dozen buttons on her new blue dress

In Zeelandia the girls go wearing

The easily shed clothes of summer: winds from the strait

Come to tease open their butterfly collars

I thought I had discovered the Spice Islands, who would have known

Rising up in front of me are still those bloodthirsty

Breasts with their hint of mint. Isla

Formosa, I come to lie upon

Your cool mattress of the wind. Isla

Formosa, I come from afar to colonize you

But have already submitted. Isla

Formosa. Isla

Formosa

January 1975

Europe

From "Naming the Reality of Chinese Criticism"

The [Chinese] philosopher of literature does not systematize his thoughts; still less does he believe in logical exposition of what he upholds as the basic truth of good literature. He implies, hints, and suggests to reveal his knowledge and taste, but he does not write an "exposition" on literature.... The nature of Chinese criticism and theory was defined by the mid-sixth century. It developed in diverse ways in the subsequent periods, and accumulated an extensive vocabulary, but its essence did not change. The educated Chinese enjoyed literary philosophy, taking delight in its ambiguity as they did in poetry and philosophy. They found it intellectually and aesthetically satisfactory.

Contemporary Chinese students of literature would probably have continued in the same vein if they had not been exposed to Western definitions of literary criticism, which seem to imply that Chinese literary philosophy, in its traditional form, can hardly become a part of the literary curriculum in a modern discipline. This skepticism has deepened in the last two decades as Chinese students who have read modern Western criticism as an aid to understanding Western classics turn to the investigation of Chinese literature. Western students, with more solid philological training in the Chinese language than their predecessors, and with a strong desire to interpret Chinese literature in the context of world literature, find that literary criticism may be the most significant topic, after poetry and fiction, investigated in the vast field of Chinese literature. These students have realized that what is called "criticism" in English studies, for example, is elusive, if not illusory, in Chinese studies....

Chinese criticism and theory are difficult to understand, modern scholars complain, because they were presented in terms and conventions accessible only to a few, and their statements were usually filled with difficult allusions. A Chinese writer of *shih-hua*, for example, would elaborate on a point he was making about a poem by comparing it with a classic, which he referred to in an abbreviated form; with a well-known work by a famous poet from

Journal of Asian Studies 38(3):529–31 (1979).

an earlier dynasty, whom he called by his style name; or with the axiom of a specific school he and his literary colleagues would recognize. He assumed that readers would share his familiarity with the classics and with other works he referred to. We cannot. Ordinarily, a *shih-hua* is intended to delight rather than to instruct its reader. We might, indeed, be delighted by the writer's witty, penetrating but cryptic remarks about a small poem if he had not filled them with inexplicable allusions to and unidentified quotes from the ocean of Chinese poetry. We yearn for a pedagogy that will equip us to understand his ideas. Unfortunately, he never thought we could be so ignorant.

蟬

我在透明的蟬聲中醒來，思索著，如今這熾熱的透明已經涵蓋了昨
夜幾分激越幾分淒楚的話題，涵蓋它如同夏天的膠囊，正適合我
囫圇吞服，无須皺眉咀嚼了

我接開窗簾，尋覓著。然而聲音如何能擔任我們急切的嚮導？除了
知識的威力，我們還相信感官，然而然而，我的挫折何嘗不是因
為我曾經訴諸錯誤的感官，訴諸那錯誤的嚮導？

據說蟬的生命很合乎悲劇英雄的典型。如此卑微遲緩，它堅忍奮鬥，
一旦脫離泥土的潤澤，便緣著樹幹游移而上。我必須歌頌它上升
的意志，寂寞勇敢的意志

在雨露中成形

經過一些粗糙的樹瘤，如同但丁夢中世界的層次。也如同虔誠篤實
的但丁，多彌尼各教派的香客，毫不猶豫地向命定的輝煌世界匍
匐前行，而輝煌是寂寞

Cicada

I awake amid the transparent buzz of cicada wings, pondering
 the scorching transparency that envelops last night's exciting
 and yet depressing topic of conversation, enveloping it in
 the gelatinous capsule of summer, perfect for swallowing
 whole, no need to chew

Opening the blinds, I search for it. But how could sound ever
 function as our eager guide? In addition to the power of our
 intellect, we must trust our senses; yet, isn't my frustration
 the result of once-mistaken senses, that mistaken guide?

They say that the life of a cicada is an apt model for the tragic
 hero. Humble and slow, it steadfastly struggles on; once
 leaving the damp mud, it follows the trunk of the tree,
 winding its way upward. I shall sing the praises of its
 ascending ambition, its lonely, brave ambition

It reaches its adult stage amidst the dew and rain

Passing through knotty burls that swirl like the circles of Dante's
 inferno. It crawls, like Dante, the devoted Dominican
 pilgrim, without faltering it crawls towards that world of
 predestined glory, but in that glory is loneliness

寂寞不可能絕對不可能進入我們超知識的話題，三分古典的犬儒本
　　色，七分浪漫的狂飆精神。昨夜我們談論民族和社會的前途，歷
　　史的型態，也嘗試去爲愛下定義……

愛是不可定義的。「譬如說，」對方分析道：「僅僅對自己的精誠
　　狂烈負責尚且將殘害別人的精誠和狂烈。短暫的執著可能比永遠
　　冷漠更可怕。你說是不是？」

我喃喃無言。第二天在透明的蟬聲中醒來，我思索著激越凄楚的民
　　族社會和歷史問題，以及愛的定義。拉開窗簾，讓聲音做嚮導，
　　我髣髴已經尋到它的位置。它曾經在雨露中成形

如今正在熾熱的嘶鳴中宣告生命旅程的終點。我髣髴已經尋到它輝
　　煌的位置，它在右前方焚燒的鳳凰木上

一九七八・八

Loneliness should never enter into our topic of conversation,

    rarefied and intellectual as it is—three parts classical and

    seven parts stormy romanticism. Last night we discussed the

    future of society and the nation, the pattern of history,

    trying to establish a definition of love . . .

Undefinable love. "For example," he said, "merely to act on

    one's devotion and passion will destroy the devotion and

    passion of another. Brief persistence can be more terrifying

    than eternal coldness, don't you agree?"

I stammer, say nothing. The next day awakening amid the

    transparent buzz of cicada wings, I ponder the exciting, yet

    depressing questions of society, nation, and history, as well

    as the definition of love. Raising the window, with sound as

    my guide, I seem to have located its position. It reaches its

    adult stage amidst the dew and rain

Its scorching call announces now that it has reached its final

    destination. I seem to have located its glorious position—

    front and right of the flaming phoenix tree

August 1978

禁忌的遊戲 1

午間
樹葉在紗窗外輕輕搖
搖一種情調，無從了解的大羅曼史
（G絃不易控制，她說。頭髮向左滑落）
垂眉看無名指困難地壓著格倫那達的風
一個修女在窗內詠誦玫瑰經，偶然抬頭
遠方正緩緩走過一匹流浪人的馬
那馬走得好慢，她已經撥完十二顆念珠了
流浪人自地平線上消逝。羅爾卡如是說……

這時靠農牧場那邊的木瓜樹
正在快速結果。午間的情調
又髣髴負載著纍纍的靜止
十二年髣髴也是靜止——
她終於學會了G絃，甚至
能夠控制那種美好的音色了

我聽到，於是我聽到苦楝一邊生長
一邊拋落果子的聲音：起初
那辭枝和觸地的時間是短促的
七年後，十二年後那距離越拉越長
（我們用春天的雨絲度量，而我
幾乎無法忍耐那一段分割的時間）

Forbidden Game 1

At noon

Leaves flutter beyond the open window

Flutter in a feeling of an unfathomable romance

(The G chord is hard to hold, she says, hair falling over her

    right shoulder)

Eyes lowered, her ring finger reaches to fret a Granadian tune

Inside the window a nun chants the Rosary, lifting her head

A lone horseman slowly passes in the distance

So slowly that she has already counted through twelve beads

Before he vanishes over the horizon. So Lorca said . . .

At this moment the papaya tree out by the ranch

Is rapidly bearing fruit. The feeling at noon

Seems to be supporting stacks of stillness

And there are also the twelve years of stillness here—

Finally she learns to play the G chord,

To finger even that beautiful note

I hear the sound then, I hear the weeping willow grow

Tossing away its seeds; in the beginning

The time between branch-leaving and earth-striking was brief

But after seven years, then twelve years, the distance grows

(We measure it out in threads of spring rain, but I

Can hardly bear the fissures of time)

苦楝垂直穿過五線譜的剎那
和剎那，點點的低低的苦苦的
一點比一點低，一點比
一點苦的聲音

而終於跌落在地上了。她擡頭
看我憂鬱地聽著聽不見的樹葉
在紗窗外輕輕地輕輕地搖——午間
一隻白貓在陽臺上瞌睡
去年冬天的枯葉擁在階前
很多年以前的枯葉堆在心裏
「終於學會了G絃」她說：「這樣子——」
微笑用無名指輕易地，草原地
壓著格倫那達的風……
詩人開門走到街心，靜止的午間
忽燃爆開一排槍聲，羅爾卡
無話可說了，如是仆倒

人們紛紛推窗探看
翻倒了好幾盆三色菫
烈日下有一棵覆地的苦楝降八度
沉默地結束了一段早夭的大羅曼史

一九七六·五

Like instants woven into a musical score

Bit by bit, deeper, and bitter too

A little bit deeper, a little more bitter

They drip

Finally falling to the ground. She raises her head

To look at me sadly, listening to the soundless leaves

Fluttering lightly outside the open window—at noon

A white cat napping on the balcony

The dried leaves of last winter gather in front of the steps

And the dried leaves of many years pile up in our hearts

"I finally have learned the G chord," she says. "Listen . . . "

With her ring finger she reaches lightly, like plains

Holding down a Granadian turn . . .

The poet opens the door and walks out into the street.

    The noon's stillness

Explodes with the sound of gunfire, Lorca

Has nothing to say, collapsing so

People push open their windows

Overturning flower pots

Under the blazing sun the weeping willow plays an octave lower

Concluding the silent romance of fallen youth

May 1976

禁忌的遊戲2

在遠遠的地方，河水因爲一場新雨
而充沛於開始轉紅的楓林後面
我能夠聽見鱒魚呼吸著彼此的
聲音，聽見晚烟報知秋天的
豐盛和落寞，然而有一種
寧靜的情緒比所有的聲音更響亮
而且更肅穆——在遠遠的
遠遠的地方

允許我又在思索時間的問題了。「音樂」
你的左手按在五線譜上說：「本來也衹是
時間的藝術。還有空間的藝術呢？
還有時間和空間結合的？還有……」
還有時間和空間，和精神結合的
飛揚上升的快樂。有時
我不能不面對一條
因新雨而充沛的河水
在楓林和晚烟之後
在寧靜之前

有時你無法尋到我的蹤跡
（即使你努力尋找）有時
夜晚正緩緩地降落在山谷這邊
一支號角在城堡裏

Forbidden Game 2

In a place far far away, a recent rain fills the river

Surging behind the stand of maples that are just turning red

I can hear the trout calling to each other

Can hear the evening mist announcing autumn's

Flourish and decline, and yet there is a

Feeling of stillness louder and clearer than all other sounds

And more solemn too—in a place far far

Far away

Allow me to consider again the question of time. "Music"

You say with your left palm resting on a score, "Is actually only

A temporal art. And is there a spatial art?

And is there an art that unites time and space? And is there . . . "

And there is a joy that soars, uniting time and space, and

Spirit too. Sometimes

I must face the

River surging with recent rain

Beyond the maples and evening mist

Before the stillness

Sometimes there is no way to follow my track

(Even if you search) sometimes

Just as evening descends here into the valley

A bugle blows resolutely

果敢地吹，我有一條路
可以直接到達死滅和永生
你可能尋到，在幻想的
草原上，在夢的邊緣
在淚在血

我難以相信，難以相信這是逝者之歌
浮沉在一些簡單動人的傳說裏
作爲謠言的伴奏（有一支號角
城堡裏吹）：人們環立傾聽
直到馬隊的蹄聲從市鎮的四面響起
而且越來越近，人們
乃無辜地散開

「是有一種時間和空間
和精神結合的快樂」詩人說：
「飛揚上升的快樂」
在遠遠的地方
河水因新雨而充沛
髣髴是寧靜
而我聽到
一種更寧靜的情緒比所有的聲音
響亮，一種淺淺的憤懑是眞實
是小小的吶喊，在夢和記憶的邊緣
在淚在血

Inside the garrison, I have a way

That leads directly to death and immortality

You might be able to follow it, in illusionary

Plains, in the border of dreams

In blood, in tears

I find it hard to believe, to believe that this is the song of the dead

Floating in simple, touching times

Playing the accompaniment to rumors (a bugle

Blows inside the garrison): people stand in a circle, listening closely

Until from all around the town the sound of hoofbeats

Comes, closer and closer, people

Then dispersing in innocence

"There is a joy that unites time, space

And spirit too," says the poet,

"A soaring joy."

In a place far far away

A river surges with recent rain

Like stillness

And I hear

A feeling of stillness louder and clearer than all other

Sounds, a shallow kind of rancor that is real

A tiny roar on the borders of dreams and memory

In blood, in tears

你如何忘懷那眞實——
通過蘆葦的籌備，星辰和
樹的私語，月和海水的
作業——如何忘懷一條街道
一些水果和酒（即使
你可以）我不能想像
那槍聲引導的死滅和永生
當我走進一片開始轉紅的
楓林，我不能想像

這是逝者之歌，浮沉在
簡單動人的傳說裏
作爲謠言的伴奏——
有一支號角
城堡裏吹

一九七六·九

How could you forget the reality of it—

Passing through reedy preparations, the secret conversations

Of the stars and trees, the assignments of

Moon and sea—how could you forget about the street

The fruit and wine (and even

If you could) I cannot imagine

The death and immortality that gunfire ushers in

When I walk into the stand of maples just

Turning red, I cannot imagine

This is the song of the dead, floating

In simple, touching times

Playing the accompaniment to rumors—

A bugle blows

Inside the garrison

September 1976

禁忌的遊戲3

試著來記取
一份偉大的關懷，在格倫那達
試著記取你們的語言和痛苦
綠色的風和綠色馬，你們的
語言和快樂——你們偶然快樂
——在河岸醒轉的樹林外
小毛驢的蹄聲，此刻，響過酒和收穫

她希望與你交談，使用多音節的單字
與你交談（也使用手勢）
她打聽教堂座落的方向
雖然這並不表示她如此年輕
就已經了解宗教的格倫那達
啊聖·麥柯，請你收留
一個善良好奇的女孩
帶她長大

教她在傾聽鐘鳴的時候
聽到一片更深的歷史底歎息
記載在教科書不顯著的地方
在橄欖窗彩色玻璃的反面——
那是農民的汗
兵士的血
教她認識河岸上一排無花果樹

Forbidden Game 3

Trying to recall

That act of compassion in Granada

Trying to recall your language and your pain

The green wind and green horses, your

Language and your joy—an occasional joy—

Beyond the woods that awake by the river

The hoofbeats of the mules rattle across the wine and harvest

She wants to converse with you in multisyllable words

To converse with you (in gestures too)

She asks directions to the church

Although this is no indication that so young she

Understands the spirituality of Granada

Saint Michael, keep her,

This good, curious girl

Raise her well

When she listens to the tolling of the bell,

Let her hear the sighs of history

Hidden in the margins of her schoolbooks

On the backside of stained glass in olive windows—

That is the sweat of farmers

The blood of warriors

Let her know about the fig grove by the river

有一陣風曾經來自集結的城堡
曾經迫害那禮拜日出門的少年
（愛情和他的小帽一樣鮮潔
他能夠背誦羅爾卡的新詩）
少年曾經臥死在這一排好看的
無花果樹下，來不及流淌
那農民的汗和兵士的血

教她傾聽並且認識這些這些

然後你可以把她還給我
一個過激的異教份子
我們將費上整個冬天
學習修辭和語意，然後
把修辭和語意忘記。我們
用一個春天的時間旅行
並且在夜晚的旅店裏討論
格倫那達的神話與詩。我們
從事田野的調查和訪問
一起渡過那漫長的暑假
搜集民歌和諺語。而秋天
將發現我們在紅葉的窗戶裏
整理著農民的汗和兵士的
血，小毛驢的蹄聲
將響過酒和收穫

How from the garrisons a wind arose

To persecute the young man who came out that Sunday

(Both love and his hat fresh and pure

He was able to recite the poems of Lorca)

The young man lies dead below the lovely

Figs, not having time to share in

The sweat of farmers, the blood of warriors

Let her hear and understand all this about all this

And later you can return her to me

This radical heathen

We will spend the whole winter

Studying rhetoric and semantics, and later

Will forget the rhetoric and semantics. We

Will use the spring to travel

And at night discuss the myths of Granada

In hotel rooms. We will

Engage in field research and interviews

And together pass the long summer vacation

Collecting folk songs and proverbs. And in the autumn

Discover that we are inside the red-leafed windows

Putting in order the sweat of farmers and the blood of

Warriors, the mule's hoofbeats

Will rattle across the wine and harvest

你將會喜愛這麼一個善良好奇的女孩
啊聖‧麥柯，試著來記取
一份偉大的關懷

一九七六‧九

You will come to adore such a good and curious girl

Saint Michael, trying to recall

That act of compassion

September 1976

禁忌的遊戲4

冷冷的陽光照亮一條承霤
好安寧：居民也許都在讀早報
沒有任何令人激動的消息
足以破壞這清晨的空白——
苟延的蚊蚋是發光的一些線條
緩緩地飛著。甚至沒有風

我坐在格倫那達的邊緣
思索著詩人流血的心
一支吉他斜置在酒店牆角
屋子裏漾著昨夜柴火的餘溫
我對自己說：「音樂最多祇是
故事的裝飾，韻律和節奏都是」
音樂逸失的時候（譬如說此刻）
故事還在，英雄栩栩若生
他一度道別的人也還在
在有花的院子裏梳頭

假如音樂真適宜為愛下定義
愛難道也是生命的裝飾而已？
我思索著，街心有幾隻灰鴿子
在散步啄食。那裏曾經流血
「愛，當愛逸失的時候（譬如說
此刻，或者明日，他年），生命

Forbidden Game 4

Cold sunlight shines on the eaves

Deadly quiet: perhaps the townsfolk are all reading the morning paper

There is no news so earthshaking

That it could obliterate the white space of dawn—

Gnats go mindlessly on, weaving threads of light

As they fly slowly round. There's no wind

I sit on the edges of Granada

Pondering the poet's bleeding heart

A guitar leans in the corner of the tavern

The warmth of last night's fire undulates across the room

I say to myself: "Music is at most only

An ornament for the story, rhyme and meter are no more than that"

When the music is lost (as it is now)

The story still goes on, the hero so lifelike

The person to whom he once said good-bye is still there

There in the flower garden combing her hair

If music is most suited to the definition of love

Could love be merely an ornament for our lives?

I ponder, in the middle of the street a few pigeons

Strut and scratch for food. There where blood once flowed

"Love, when love is lost (as it is

Now, tomorrow, or in another time)

還有可能繼續？」有人堅持
愛乃是生命的全部

我思索著，坐在
格倫那達的邊緣
一匹毛驢自街道那頭走來
後面跟著一名惺忪的男子——
他昨夜曾經散佈了六個謠言。然而
「愛逸失的時候，生命應當還可以
完成。」我快樂地朝向這個結論進行
英雄還在學習越野和爆破
即使他在異鄉陣亡，或僅祗
被早晨的馬隊格殺，那一度躍動的
生命活在比格倫那達更遠的地方
他一度道別的人也還在
在有花的院子裏梳頭

這個結論使我感覺滿意
撞頭看冷冷的陽光照亮
一條承霤，推桌起立
有人拾起屋角的那支吉他
重覆著遙遠遙遠的大羅曼史
我喜悅地走向鴿子啄食的地方
那名趕毛驢的男子（他昨夜
已經散佈了六個有關於我的謠言）

Can we still go on?" Some insist

That love is all there is

I ponder, sitting

On the edges of Granada

A burro coming down the street

Followed by a bleary-eyed boy—

Last night he spread rumors, six of them. But

"When love is lost, life can still be

Fulfilling." I move joyfully toward this conclusion

The hero still studies cross-country travel and demolitions

Even if he is killed in combat in another land, or merely

Executed by the Civil Guard in the morning he still

Lives on in a place far far from Granada

The one to whom he says good-bye is still there

There in the flower garden combing her hair

I find great satisfaction with this conclusion

I raise my head to look at the cold sunlight shining

On the eaves, pushing back the table I stand

Someone picks up the guitar from the corner of the room

Singing again the romance of far far away

I walk out to where the pigeons strut and scratch for food

The boy driving the burro (last night he

Had spread rumors about me, six of them)

回頭對我招呼，惺忪地——
吉他聲忽然中斷

一排槍聲……

一九七六·十

Turns to call to me, bleary-eyed—

The sound of the guitar interrupted

By gunfire . . .

October 1976

一位英國文學教授之死

我聽說那是離島的清晨，最困難的
一刻，他的消逸猶似島之沉没
進入我有限的知識中。而我，我因爲
聽到他的死訊而辨明離島的方位
在夢之西南方，現實之東北方——喪鐘緩緩敲著
鐘爲亞瑟·奧柏格，爲你，爲我敲

我還記得亞瑟·奧柏格穿著歐戰風情的雨衣
在一棵點滴不已的大橡樹下和我談論
玄學詩人。亞瑟·奧柏格有一雙明亮的
大眼睛，其餘的都已不可形容了
而那最困難的一刻是離島的，離島的清晨
我轉向地圖去尋找他自殺的時間和空間

在浮橋碼頭的附近
黎明背後
我聽說
他留下一首長詩

一九七七·五

On the Death of a Professor
of British Literature

I hear that it was daybreak on a coastal island, the most difficult

Hour, his loss is like the sinking of an island

Entering into my limited knowledge. And, hearing

The news of his death, I calculate the exact location of the coastal island

Southwest of dreams, northeast of reality—the funeral bell slowly tolls

The bell tolls for Arthur, tolls for thee, and tolls for me

I still remember Arthur in a trench coat like those of the Great War

Discussing with me below an oak tree that still dripped with rain

The metaphysical poets. He had large

Shining eyes, the rest I can't describe

And the most difficult hour was daybreak, daybreak on a coastal island

I turn away to plot the exact time and place of his suicide

Near the floating dock

Behind the early morning light

He left behind a long poem

So I hear

May 1977

班吉夏山谷

為紀念一位阿富汗朋友而作。他曾經對我
說：「班吉夏山谷美得像中國女子的眼睛。」

在班吉夏山谷
當春天隨我的族人撤退了，我們
知道敵人和豪雨一樣都在高原上
集結。我們知道因為我們曾經
穿戴濕濕的布衣帽奔跑於
泥濘的草原和街道：春天
屬於我們，夏天也屬於
我們，班吉夏山谷的歲月
屬於我們。在班吉夏山谷當春天
暫時離去，草木比去年長得更好
或許是硝煙和毒氣的
滋養，戰爭的緣故——
而我還聽得見族人游走的足音
零星的槍聲不斷，狙擊於
正午，黃昏，黎明

他們在班吉夏山谷佈置了
佔領軍總部和無數的哨崗
紅軍在村莊裏外結伴巡邏
我的族人沉默地觀看
並且鋸著木頭，剝著豆
在井邊汲水，燠熱的空氣裏

The Panjshir Valley

Written in memory of an Afghan friend who once said,
"The Panjshir Valley is as beautiful as the eyes of a Chinese woman."

In the Panjshir Valley

When spring followed my people in retreat, we

Knew the enemy, like the rains, had amassed troops

On the plain. We knew because we ran along

Muddy roads and through fields

In cotton clothes soaking wet: spring

Belongs to us, summer belongs to

Us, Panjshir Valley time

Belongs to us. When spring left the Panjshir

For a time, the plants grew more than last year

Perhaps they were nourished by gunfire

And mustard gas, perhaps it is because of the war—

But I still can hear the sound of my people's retreat

Sporadic but incessant gunfire, snipers

At noon, dawn, and dusk

In the Panjshir Valley the Soviets set up

Their headquarters and countless outposts

And sent patrols into the villages and fields

While my people watched in silence

And sawed wood, shucked beans

And drew water from the well, suddenly an infant's cry

忽然拔起嬰兒的哭聲
我的族人在屈辱中工作
在哭聲裏活。他們沒有淚
乾燥的班吉夏山谷
盤旋著三兩隻鷹
蛇在岩石和沙礫間流竄，蜈蚣和
蜥蜴吮盡死者身上最後一滴血

大半，我大半族人在班吉夏山谷
在通向安德拉布的狹路間埋伏
他們趁濃密的夜色摸近敵人的
營盤，緊靠著童年放牧的故鄉
並且點發一些火箭，攻擊
佔領軍的車隊，時常是在
破曉以前，炮聲撕裂沉睡的大地
他們沒有番號，在乾燥的
丘陵和矮樹林中奔跑
直昇機的螺旋槳由遠而近
機關槍掃射我們放牧的草原
如豪雨打過夢境，然而
春天將屬於我們，夏天也屬於
我們，當草木越長越茂盛
羊群還要和我們的孩子一樣的
在哭聲中長大，充滿這屬於
我們的，完全屬於我們的
班吉夏山谷

一九八四

Pierced the scorching air

My people work amidst disgrace

Live in the sound of weeping. They have no more tears

Above the parched valley

Three eagles soar

Snakes slither through the boulders, centipedes and

Lizards sip the last drops of blood from the bodies of the dead

Most of my people are in the Panjshir Valley

Lying in ambush along the narrow road through Anjuman

Under the cover of heavy night they infiltrate the encampments

Of the enemy, and fire mortars

Close to where as children they herded sheep

Truck convoys explode, often before

Dawn, the sound rips open the sleeping earth

They belong to no unit, running through

The parched hills and scrub trees

The helicopter rotors closing in

Machine guns strafe the plains where we herded sheep

Falling like rain into a dream, but

Spring will belong to us, summer will belong

To us, when the trees and grass grow taller and more lush

The flocks of sheep, like our children

Will grow up in the sound of weeping, filling

This valley that belongs to us, belongs only to us

The Panjshir

1984

九　辯

2　迂迴行過

春天，我迂迴行過
鷓鴣低呼的森林
搜尋預言裏
多湖泊的草原，多魚
多小風，多繁殖的夢
多神話。我在搜尋

風在我攫捕的臂彎
柔軟如可哀的江南
在短暫的歷史裏
搖曳是臨水的荷芰

夏天，夏天在
我營建的小園停留
成熟膨脹。她穿著橘花
易落的衣裳，鮮紅的
櫻桃小鞋，頭上戴
枇杷一頂遮陽帽
我知道了，我為她
預備一張湖綠的床
鯉魚枕頭，繁星編織
晚間輕輕的被褥

From "Nine Arguments"

2. Meandering

In spring I go meandering through

The forest of low cooing doves

Seeking the promised

Grasslands with their many lakes, many fish

And many breezes, the reproductive dreams

The many myths. I am seeking

The wind in my embrace

Soft as the South in all its sorrow

In its brief moment in history

Quivering by the water's edge, the lotus

In summer, the summer

Lingers, matures, and grows full-bodied

In the garden of my making. She wears the clothes

Of orange blossoms easily shed, slippers

Of cherries, and on her head

A loquat hat wide-brimmed against the sun

Knowing this, I prepare

For her a bed of laken green

A pillow of snowy carp, and bedding lightly

Woven out of evening stars

我知道我已經留下她
夢是鷦鴣的言語
風是湖泊的姿態
魚是神話的起源
臨水的荷芰搖曳
青青是倒影

一九七八

I know I have kept her here

Dreams are the conversation of doves

Wind, the posture of lakes

And fish, the source of myths

At the water's edge the lotus quivers

Green and blue are its reflections

1978

In the Kuroshio Current

From "The Nature of Narrative in T'ang Poetry"

"Lament of a Ch'in Woman" is not merely a solid narrative account telling of the fall of the T'ang dynasty; it is also magnificent poetry. The dynamism of its lucid, flowing style generates and sustains the progress of the poem. The sure mastery with which its incidents are successively arrayed proves, probably for the first time in Chinese literature, that the heptasyllabic verse is capable of extended narration without slipping into either extravagantly ornamented poetic diction or flatness. The poem is free of the dense diction or constrained obscurity that characterize many literati works written in the late T'ang period. At the same time, it avoids the monotonous rhyme patterns found in most of the folk and religious pieces uncovered in Tun-huang, many of them roughly contemporary to Wei Chuang's work. Wei Chuang demonstrates that heptasyllabic verse is still powerful enough to combine the strength of the literati and the folk styles of narrative poetry, in an exuberant yet succinct and straightforward presentation of the plot. Two thousand years of slow but steady development of the form sustains Wei Chuang's alternation of plot-advancing elements with the display of picturesque and emotional moments; such alternation enriches the texture of the narrative while minimizing the danger of dullness. No line or passage fails to contribute to the general effect of the poem as a testimony of the catastrophe of an empire and, above all, as an affirmation of the woman as the true heroine of a grand tale. Indeed, her sisters have always been heroines in the folk tradition of narrative poetry....

The heroic adventure of the Ch'in woman is the primary theme in the plot of the poem. The national catastrophe serves as a backdrop, the old man's plaint as a supplement, and the poet's attention, a silent comment. In the process of the plot's unfolding the characterization of the heroine is fulfilled. The naive tone that marks her first reaction to the assault of the rebels dissolves with the description of the violent treatment she and other women re-

In *The Vitality of the Lyric Voice: Shih Poetry from the Late Han to the T'ang*, ed. Shuen-fu Lin and Stephen Owen (Princeton: Princeton University Press, 1986), 249–50.

ceived in its aftermath—she immediately assumes a stern voice to describe the starvation that followed the fall of the capital. The poignant lyricism in the transition indicates the growth of a feminine will to protest. When she assumes the authority to interpret the humiliation of the god, who fled the temple to hide himself from the human cataclysm, she becomes a Cassandra, released from all ethical codes to move in a fantastic realm. But the desperate, mystic tone subsides after she listens to the old man's story and realizes that the woe she has witnessed is a universal one. At that moment she matures, so much so that the concluding passage, in which she expresses her determination to proceed south, is narrated most calmly, careful to distinguish hearsay and true information, to weigh the pros and cons of seeking a foreign shelter and, in the gracious language that marks her gentle breeding, to encourage the listeners of her lament to consider joining the exodus. Wei Chuang has successfully portrayed a woman with distinctive temperament, love, and hatred who, having experienced violence, hunger, and inclemency, is as tragically resolute as her sisters in earlier narrative poetry. She is ready to abandon her homeland, the old Ch'ang-an, now in ruins, a city which we know in retrospect has never returned to its former grandeur and perhaps never will.

會　話

這件事發生在普林士頓
春雨似乎是停了又髣髴
還細微飄飄而淡淡的烟
浮遠浮近在林木的末梢
我正坐在窗口等候張望
不知道你在學校裏怎樣

紅頸子的小鳥在草地上
踏過一叢叢的新葱覓食
院子裏很靜而我在窗口
喝茶吸烟讀涉江的屈原
不斷擡頭看窗外而你在
學校喝咖啡且英文會話

網球場上有老人在溜狗
春雨似乎已經停了否則
你沒帶傘下課怎麼樣走
英文會話能應付就行了
我把書推開張望你的車
只要你平安回家就行了

一九七九・四・四

Conversation Class

And so here at Princeton

The spring rain seems to have stopped but

It might still be drizzling, a light mist

Floats here and there on the tips of the woods

As I sit in the window waiting and watching

Wondering what you are doing still at school

On the lawn a robin hops through clumps of

Spring leeks looking for food

The yard is quiet and I am in the window

Drinking tea, smoking, and reading exiled Ch'ü Yüan

Lifting my eyes every few seconds to look and you

Are at school drinking coffee and speaking English

Out by the tennis court an old man walking his dog

The spring rain seems to have stopped otherwise

What will you do after class without your umbrella

As long as you can get by with English that's all that matters

I push away the book and watch for your car

Just as long as you get home safely that's all that matters

April 4, 1979

子午協奏曲

1

方才過了子夜。我曾凝視紅色的秒針趕到
聽千萬座自鳴鐘齊響，遠方島上
炎熱的午後從多汗的涼蓆上小夢
醒來，修長清癯的小母親
痴心愛笑，羞澀的情人

陽光如猛虎的顏色……
月影幽微，落在短牆上
躡足像鄰居的白貓沿丁香枝頭行走

2

我在隔簾的風聲裏等候，聽見
淋浴的水龍撲打你健康的肩胛
洪荒的思念循時空的神話系統飛落
撕攫的五爪猶帶獻身的柔情
一種柔情，在四更的沉寂裏
撫愛東南屋角一顆全裸的星

風向有些猶疑
海洋沉睡如兒子

The International Dateline Concerto

1

Just after midnight. I stare at the luminous second hand rushing on

Listening to a million clocks on that faraway island chime in unison

She awakes from a dream, lying on a cool mat in the stifling heat of the

Afternoon, the young mother, tall and slender

My lover, shy, infatuated, and full of fun

The sunlight is the color of a Bengal tiger

The cast of the moon is faint, falling on the wall

Tiptoeing along the lilac branches like the neighbor's white cat

2

I wait in the wind on the other side of the curtain, listening

To the shower pummel her strong back

Primitive urges fly along the myth system of time and space

Bloody claws still carry the softness of a body proffered

A softness that in the stillness of the deep night

Caresses the naked star in the southeast corner of the room

The direction of the wind keeps changing

The sea sleeps as soundly as our son

我側身躺臥等候，默誦更漏子
聽水聲喧嘩如閃爍的龍鱗
溫存地沖洗你的肩胛和四肢
一點點刺痛。你感覺何如？何如
我放心的擁抱？微微呼喊的
是懷裏一顆全裸的星

風向有些猶疑
海洋沉睡如兒子

水珠從額頭和雙頰滴落
我仰臉想見你著急地眨眼
在四更沉寂的枕上，聽你悉悉哼著小歌
擦拭頭髮和發亮的身體，忽然
陽臺外飛落一場成熟的暴雨
再擡頭，屋頂上飄浮著
濃烈的水蒸氣
淡淡的烟

　　3
天微微明，呼晨的鳥聲悠悠如髮
如你乾燥的髮上沾我躭舌淋漓的汗
片刻濕透了耳根，啁啁啾啾
飛禽蔽空飛臨一浩浩的長河
衝刺水花的石瀨，淺灘，漩渦
我在破曉的天候裏觀察你
以羽翼兒猛的翻飛

I lie on my side in wait, quietly singing the "Clepsydra Song"

Listening to the water murmur like the scales of a dragon

Glittering warmly over your back and down your limbs

Stinging a little. How does it feel?

Like when I hold you in my arms? Softly moaning

The star naked in my embrace

The direction of the wind keeps changing

The sea sleeps as soundly as our son

Beads of water drip from your forehead and cheeks

I raise my head, wishing I could see you blink them away

On the pillow of the deep night, I listen to you softly hum a tune

Wiping dry your hair and body glowing, suddenly

Out on the balcony a mature rain pours down

I raise my head again, on the ceiling floats

Heavy steam

A light mist

3

The sky is turning light, the songs of the morning birds are like your hair

Like your hair damp again with my sweat, its dripping southern accent

For a moment soaking your temples, chirping and calling

Birds on wing fill the sky nearing the mighty river

Riffles interlaced with water flowers, the submerged beach, the whirlpool

I wait in the sky at the break of day observing you

With frantic flapping wings

此刻在遠方，黑夜
方才降落，没有聲息的夜
剛剛降落到你的短袖單衣上

你的耳根濕透如水仙
頭後的寒毛在河岸風中憻慄
眉如縠紋，眼是亢奮不息的深潭
搖盪著亙古魚龍的夢。是的在廣大的
樹影下，眼是洶湧飛濺的古潭
隨我羽翼拍打的狂風而震撼
是的在廣大的樹影下

狂風掀動你不能休息的鼻翅
以蛺蝶的喜悅輕輕反擊。天將大明
你微張的唇溫暖而潮濕——
黑夜方才降落到你的唇
一艘載著香料水果和樂器的船

　　4
我依次將百葉窗打開
像打開一排精緻的紐扣
豐滿的夏日依偎我
以早晨的艷陽抵觸我的枕頭
我翻身靠近湧動的光影，澎湃
如你的胸乳，閉眼思索，此刻
你已進入暗夜的中心，夢的森林

At this time far away, the black night

Has just fallen, the night without sound

Has just fallen into your thin summer blouse

Your temples are soaked like narcissus

The hairs on the back of your neck tremble in the river wind

Your eyebrows are silken ripples, eyes deep restless pools

Undulating with the dreams of the primeval water dragon. Yes, under the

Trees' spreading shade, your eyes are ancient pools rolling with whitecaps

Shaking in the wild wind of my beating wings

Yes, under the trees' spreading shade

The wild wind flows through your fluttering nostrils

Resisting with its butterfly joy. The day is about to break

Your parted lips are warm and moist—

The dark night has fallen upon them

A boat carrying spice, fruit, and musical scores

4

Onc by onc I open the venetian blinds

Like a row of exquisite buttons

The well-developed summer sun clings to me

Reaching down with voluptuous rays to caress my pillow

I roll over to cuddle up to her surging shadows and light

Swelling like your breasts, with eyes closed knowing that you have

Just now entered into the heart of night, the forest of dreams

白楊樹急急敲著迷失的風
在被褥上搬弄
顛倒的雙魚星座
你莫非在夢裏哭？
我聽到了，看見陽光
在我的手腕下抽搐
如激動的魚
迷失漩渦中

     5

我想以這樣的音色持續地
持續地讚美你，如蕨薇讚美肥沃的
大地，青梨在盛夏的園子裏默默
默默將果實膨脹。你的乳房勇健如七月之梨

甚至是羞澀的，在苜蓿喧呶的草地上
隱藏著，在露水耳語的草地上。我想
以這樣的音色——當日光忽然傾斜
持續地，以這樣的音色讚美你

     6

持續地，計算你安詳的呼息
當烈日停止在午後的欄杆上
一排火紅的慾望，如你清晨下床
手臂上印著的，涼蓆的痕迹

The white birch beats frantically against the wayward wind

Flitting across the bedding

The tail-to-mouth constellation of Pisces

Weren't you crying in your dream?

I heard it, looking at the rays of sunlight

Twitch underneath my wrist

Like an excited fish

Caught in a whirlpool

5

I want to praise you with this voice continuously

Continue to praise you as the ferns praise the fertile

Earth, the young peaches in the garden grow silently plump

Silent in the height of summer. Your breasts are full like July peaches

Even such a bashful one, in the field of clamorous clover

Hiding, in the field of dewy whispers. I want

With this voice—when the sun suddenly descends—

To continue with this voice to praise you

6

Continue to count your calm breathing

When the hot sun holds over the afternoon railings

A palisade of red desire, like the patterns on your arm

From the tatami when you get up in the morning

你對著展現的鏡子梳頭
汗水從胸口滑落圓圓的臍
沉默的陶甕在壁爐架上
追憶三月帶雨的蘋果花
我從鏡子的反射裏看見，在遠方島上
汗水滑落——滑落驚異的小松鼠臉上

新筍在牆角苦苦地抽芽
蚊蚋繞著溫度計飛
藍天與蒲公英在院子裏
堅持，剪草機加以化解
四鄰在洒水
天慢慢黑了

7

黑夜從海上來，閃過暗礁和石岬
踏魚的泡泡和彩霞的容貌，從海上
從群島和群島的後面，鯨魚的家鄉
掠過氣象臺的衛星和汽球，飄落在
我們臥房的窗。一盞燈照亮兩朵海棠
血紅璀燦，在我掌下手指間

而這時，在更遠更遠方的島上
我可以想像你亭午的坐姿
曾經是我努力墾拓的疆土

In front of the illuminated mirror, you comb your hair

Rivulets of sweat run down your breast into your round navel

The silent porcelain vase stands above the fireplace

Recalling the rain-soaked apple blossoms of March

I see from my reflection in the mirror, on that faraway island

Rivulets of sweat running down—running down the squirrel's face

In the corner of the yard the bamboo sends up hard shoots

Mosquitoes fly round and round the thermometer

There is the persistence of blue sky and dandelions

In the yard that the lawnmower will dissolve

The neighbors are all watering

The sky grows dark

7

The dark night comes in from the sea, dodging the shoals and headlands

Treading along fish bubbles and the evening glow, from the sea

From the archipelago, and from beyond the archipelago, the home
    of whales

Sliding by satellites and weather balloons, floating down

Onto the window of our bedroom. A lamp shines on twin begonia
    clusters

Glistening blood-red under my palm, between my fingers

And just now, on the island far far away

I can imagine the way you sit there at midday

I have sought new territory for cultivation

豐富的水源在大地上流，說它是汗
其實是洶湧璀燦的血脈，灌溉
你戀慕的海棠，在我掌下手指間

我俯身向你美麗的腰腹
有力的絲絨比春日還長
遮蓋我探索的眼睛——
亭午，所有風都在橋下睡眠
我是熱心的騎者，尋覓著命運的
海棠，海棠在我掌下手指間

尋覓，在廣濶的石岬和暗礁之間
北溫帶的藤蔓垂落靜止的水面
鮭魚在深海底下孵化，嚮往
我們家族的呼聲，顏色鮮明
如你開放的海棠，在我掌下手指間

8

你在擦拭著午睡的眠床了，眼睛瞇成
含羞草。此刻，夜已經越積越深了
在飄著涼風的陽臺上，我獨自寧靜
試看七月繁複的星象——思索著
宇宙的奧秘尚且不如你慵懶的神情
更令我在夜色中因竹葉的細語叮嚀
而逐漸由寧靜轉爲焦躁，如航海的人
迷失了追尋的方向，北斗也是枉然

The abundant springs flow out across the earth, you might say it is
  sweat
But actually it is the surging, glistening blood lines, irrigating
Your coveted begonia, under my palm, between my fingers

I lean over your beautiful belly
Its heavy velvet softer than a spring day
Covering my exploring eyes—
At midday, all the wind is sleeping under the bridge
I am the passionate horseman, seeking begonias
Of fortune, the begonias are under my palm, between my fingers

Seeking, among the headlands and shoals
Vines of the temperate zone touch the still water
Deep below in the sea salmon spawn, yearning for
Our family cry, brightly colored
Like your blossoming begonia, under my palm, between my fingers

8

You brush off the bed for your noon nap, eyes half-closed in the shape
Of the sensitive mimosa leaf. Night has grown heavier and deeper
On the balcony where the wind blows, I am alone, tranquil
Looking at the pattern of stars in the July sky—pondering
More than the profound mystery of the universe, your languorous looks
Within the whispered excitement of the night bamboo
Gradually turns my tranquility into restlessness, like
That of men lost at sea, even the North Star is useless

我看到你涉水的雙足
慢慢乾了，在遙遠的床尾
在我淡淡的燈影下。沉睡的丘陵
猶見一匹快馬在蘆花當中奔跑
月光照在蘆花映滿的馬背
馬背上一帶刀的女子
堅決保護著她的襁褓

汗水流下小腿
海洋嘹亮如兒子

我幾乎可以詮釋你夢中的旅程了
馬匹馳騁在落滿月光的蘆花當中
從一座丘陵馳向另一座丘陵
我專注地，甚至可以感覺
你如何催趕著你的坐騎
以兩腿夾擊的力

露水棲息在草地上了
海洋嘹亮如兒子

你在午睡的眠床上轉側，鬢髮汗濕
如深夜的小苜蓿，在月光的庭院
開放傳奇的白花，照見你的呼息
比我血中的洪流還急，在竹葉的
叮嚀下，七月的星象埋没霧裏

I see that your feet wet from wading in the river

Are slowly drying at the foot of that faraway bed

Under the shadows of my faint lamp. Among the rolling hills in deep

    sleep

A strong horse can still be seen galloping through the flowering rushes

The moonlight shining on its back covered with their reflection

And on his back a women with a sword

Staunchly protecting her child-in-arms

The sweat runs down her calves

The sea is as resonant as our son's voice

I could almost annotate the itinerary of your dream

The horse gallops through the flowering rushes soaked in moonlight

It gallops from one hillock to the next

Devotedly, I can even feel

How you urge on your mount

With the pressure of your thighs

Dew alights on the lawn

The sea is as resonant as our son's voice

You roll over in your noon nap, your temples damp with sweat

Like the short clover of the night, in the moonlit courtyard

White blossoms of a romance, show how your breathing

Is more agitated than the flowing of my blood, with the bamboo's

Urging, the stars of the July night sink into the fog

我把窗簾拉滿，聽你夢中低喊
我們曾經相逢於狂亂的漩渦。漩渦
在子午線那一邊，這邊是我們的王國

     9

方才過了子夜。我曾凝視紅色的秒針趕到
聽千萬座自鳴鐘齊響，遠方島上
炎熱的午後從多汗的涼蓆上小夢
醒來，修長清瘦的小母親
痴心愛笑，羞澀的情人

陽光如猛虎的顏色……
月影幽微，落在短牆上
躡足像鄰居的白貓沿丁香枝頭行走

一九八〇·七

I close the drapes, listening to you moan softly in your dream

Our whirlwind of passion first arose on that side

Of the international dateline, but here is our kingdom

9

Just after midnight. I stare at the luminous second hand rushing on

Listening to a million clocks on that faraway island chime in unison

She awakes from a dream, lying on a cool mat in the stifling heat of the

Afternoon, the young mother, tall and slender

My lover, shy, infatuated, and full of fun

The sunlight is the color of a Bengal tiger

The cast of the moon is faint, falling on the wall

Tiptoeing along the lilac branches like the neighbor's white cat

July 1980

給名名的十四行詩

1

一些些風雨之後，強大的
日光照醒苜蓿，地丁，蕨薇
我們相扶持走過草地，巡視
潮溼的圍牆，發散著早春的
氣味，往朝北朝西的方向
移植一棵冬青，順手將角門
釘牢。然後又是徹夜的風雨
在我們生命巨大的古琴上
拉緊預言的絃，張開一片恢弘
嚴肅崇高，豐盈的三月天
我們在凌晨的小寒中依偎
互相期許等待，傾聽最遠處
雨雲在海面漸漸聚集，分裂：
莊麗的號角聲，準確的鼓點

11

風也吹向山谷，河水來自
原始的寧靜。刺青，鳴蟬
那是我們秘密的世界，充滿
無遠而弗屆，不是你有限的
粉蠟筆所能夠描摹，有一種
焚身的熾熱，從童年的彼端
傳來，曾在我生涯裏挫折冷卻

From "Fourteen Sonnets for Ming-ming"

1

Following the gentle wind, the sun's

Powerful rays stir the clover, ground cover, and ferns

And we go for a walk, you in my arms, across the lawn

Inspecting the damp fence that exudes the sweet smell of early

Spring, off we go toward the north, toward the west

To transplant the holly tree, at the same time nailing shut

The side gate. Then another night of rain and wind

Tightens the strings of prediction on the zither of

Our lives, bringing in the magnificent

Serious and lofty, those fulsome days of March

When we cling to each other in the chill of the early morning

Waiting, listening intently

To the rain and clouds that gather out over the ocean, splitting:

The majestic bugle, the precise drumroll.

11

And the wind blows through the mountain gorge, the river emerges from

Primeval stillness. Tattoos and the cicada's call

Are our secret world, pervading

And stretching to the horizons, not something

You can trace with your limited crayons, a

Scorching heat coming from the far side of

Youth, frustrated and dampened in my life

又導回童年的此端，熾熱如昔
你不必畏懼，往檳榔樹開花的
方向走去，使用簡單的方言
有禮親善的手勢，在適當的
場合，以微笑回報族人的好奇
他們將擁戴你如部落的兄弟
故鄉，我們不可凌辱的土地

一九八〇

Leading on to youth here, the heat as before

But don't be frightened, walking toward the flowers of the

Betel nut tree, with simple words of the dialect,

Polite, intimate gestures, at the proper

Occasions, answering the curiosity of our ancestors with a smile

They will take care of you as a brother of the tribe

Our hometown, the land that we shall not disgrace

1980

關山月

光分玉塞古今愁

　　　　— 　翁綬

草從關外黃
月向海水借來亙古的朗亮
那纍纍發光的不是軍帳，不是牛羊
沉默的風岩如小雷，向關內低迴流盪

陰風穿梭女牆
斷續訴說血的睥睨
箭矢徒然錚鏦，干戈靜處
依然覆著許多白露寒霜
征人的眼神疲憊，茫然
鶴鳴于垤，閨中的歎息……
噩耗是晚秋零雁
在有史的那些年代
大半失落於風，於雨
於權術和欺瞞。然則
春來石榴錯落紅著
訴說血的睥睨，遠方
陰風斷續在女牆外穿梭

　　　　在閨裏閨外穿梭
低飛過枯草和亂石
愚昧的烽火臺

Moon over Pass Mountain

Rays of moonlight straddle the border pass with melancholy old and new
—Weng Shou

Out from the pass the steppes lie bleak and sere

From the sea the silvery moon borrows its ancient glow

The glittering mounds are not army tents, or flocks of sheep

In from the passes the silent wind-blown rocks like distant thunder roll

The dark wind scuttles through the parapets

Intermittently telling of the bloodied battlements

Arrows clink against stone in vain, while weapons lie quiet

Blanketed with frozen dew and crystal frost again

The eyes of the troops exhausted and perplexed

A crane alights on the rise, in her room a sigh . . .

The news of his death is the lone autumn goose

In those years full of history

Most were lost to the wind, to the rain

To court intrigues and deceptions. Otherwise

With spring the scattered pomegranates redden

Telling of the bloodied battlements, in the distance

The dark wind intermittently scuttles through the parapets

                                    Scuttles in and out of her room

Blowing lowly through the dry grass and scattered stones

The ignorant beacon tower

月下悄悄抖索
檄文，鐵蹄，衝突
腐朽的鎧甲，白骨，刁斗
在刁斗的餘音裏，小雷流盪

月向海水中藏
草從關外銜來廣大的蒼黃
那突兀的不是軍帳，不是牛羊
沉默的風岩纍纍，向關內延長

一九八二‧三

Trembles in the moonlight

Declarations of war, conflicts, horseshoes,

Encrusted armor, white bones, and kettledrums

In the echoes of the drums, the distant thunder rolls

The moon hides away in the sleepy sea

Out from the pass the steppes hold a dusky stain

Those are not army tents, or flocks of sheep

Silent wind-blown rocks spread mounded into the plain

March 1982

俯　　視

（立霧溪一九八三）

> For I have learned
> To look on nature, not as in the hour
> Of thoughtless youth, but hearing oftentimes
> The still, sad music of humanity,
> Nor harsh nor grating, though of ample power
> To chasten and subdue....
>
> —Wordsworth

假如這一次悉以你的觀點爲準

深沉的太虛幻象在千尺下反光

輕呼我的名字：仰望

你必然看到我正傾斜

我倖存之軀，前額因感動

泛發著微汗，兩臂因平衡和理性的

堅持。你是認識我的

雖然和高處的草木一樣

我的頭髮在許多風雨和霜雪以後——

不像高處的草木由繁榮渡向枯槁

已舉向歲月再生的團圓

——我的兩鬢已殘，即使不比前世

邂逅分離那時刻斑白。你認識我

嚴峻之臉是爲了掩飾羞澀

這樣俯視著山河凝聚的因緣

浮雲是飛散的衣裳，泉水滑落成澗

太陽透過薄寒照亮你踞臥之姿

Gazing Down

(Li-wu Creek, Toroko Gorge, 1983)

> For I have learned
> To look on nature, not as in the hour
> Of thoughtless youth, but hearing oftentimes
> The still, sad music of humanity,
> Nor harsh nor grating, though of ample power
> To chasten and subdue. . . .
>   —Wordsworth

If for once we accept your point of view

The dream glittering one thousand feet below

Whispering my name, gazing up

You will be certain to see my body reclining

In the lap of fortune, emotion floating

Perspiration lightly on my brow, for balance and reason my arms

Upholding. You do recognize me

Although like the grass on high ridges

After so much wind and rain, frost and snow—

Not like the grass on high ridges turning from flower to straw

Rising toward the circle born again of time—

My temples are gray, even though they are not as flecked with white

As at our meeting and parting in that other incarnation. You recognize me

My stern looks are meant to hide my embarrassment

The karma that brings me to look down on where your ridges fold

 into rivers

Clouds are clothes spread out against the sky, springs cascade

 into brooks

The sun pierces the coolness to illuminate your thighs spread wide

時常是不寧的，以斷崖的龒紋
磐石之色，充滿水份的兼葭風采
提醒我如何跋涉長路
穿過拂逆和排斥
這樣靠近你。
以最初的戀慕和燃燒的冷淡
彷彿不曾思想過的無情的心
向千尺下反光的太虛幻像
疾急發落——
如蒼鷹
切過賁張的陰涼，感覺
即使每一度造訪
都揭去一層陌生的地衣
那曾經刻在太古的肌膚上的曾經是熟悉
即使我的精神因人間的動亂而猶疑
有時不免躊躇於狂喜和悲憫之間
每一度造訪都感覺那是
陌生而熟悉，接納我復埋怨著我的你
以千層磊磊之眼
以季節的鼻息
燕雀喧鳴，和出水之貝
我這樣靠近你，俯視激情的
回聲從甚麼方向傳來，輕呼
你的名字，你正仰望我倖存之軀
這樣傾斜下來，如亢龍
向千尺下反光的太虛幻象
疾急飛落，依約探索你的源頭

Forever trembling, with the striations of rock

The hue of boulders, the charm of succulent reeds

You remind me how I have made this trek,

Penetrated resistance and rejection

To be near you like this

With the oldest devotion, burning ice

Like the emotionless heart without reflection

Toward the dream glittering one thousand feet below

I swiftly plunge—

A black hawk

Slicing through the pulsing shade, feeling that

Even though each discreet visit

Peels off another grassy layer

What is engraved in the flesh of antiquity is familiar

Even though human turmoil brings doubt to my soul

Sometimes one cannot help but hesitate between ecstasy and empathy

With each discreet inquiry feeling that it is

Strange and familiar, you who accept me and resent me

With eyes in a thousand stony layers

With the breath of the seasons

The calls of sparrow and swallow, shells lifted up from the ocean

To be near you like this

To gaze down on the echoes that rise to me from below, whispering

Your name, you are now looking up at my body in the lap of fortune

Reclining like this, the soaring, homesick dragon

Towards the dream glittering one thousand feet below

I swiftly plunge, exploring your headwaters

逼向没有人來過的地心
熾熱的火焰在冰湖上燒
那是最初，我們遭遇在
記憶的經緯線上不可辨識的一點，
復在雷霆聲中失去了彼此
我飄泊歸來，你踞臥不寧
仰望著，是的，假如這一次
悉以你的觀點爲準，這一次
當我傾一倖存之軀瀕臨，俯視……

一九八四

Working toward the core where no one has gone before

Hot flames burning into the frozen lake

That first time, we met

At an undiscernible spot on the coordinates of our memory

And then lost each other amidst the pounding thunder

I have drifted back to you, your thighs spread wide and trembling

Looking up, yes, if for once

We accept your point of view, for once

When I lean close with my body in the lap of fortune, gazing down . . .

1984

昨天的雪的歌

昨天當它降到山腰的時候，那雪線
（在陰暗的午後）我感覺它已經接近了我
並且繼續下沉，乃有飛白落在暗綠的
針葉林梢，一種指引，宇宙之慾
百葉窗外棲著幾點殘葉兩隻寒禽
所有的煙囪都靜靜沒有火氣
當那雪線終於降到山腰的時候
人們都還在趕路，從嶺外回來
車頂上架著雪橇和冰屐，我這樣
隨意想像，猜測大約就是這樣因為
它已經降到山腰六百英尺的位置，昨天
常我也隨意這樣想像著往下滑落
耳邊聽見河海之聲，欲行又止的
風，以及間斷自下一條街傳來的電鋸

電鋸？那是秋天未完成的工作它在
寒流中勤奮繼續，如饕餮之牙
夏天以前沒有完成的工作，它在
落葉的纖維裏凶狠地咬嚙，如感官
追蹤一束紅巾綢繆的髮
明快的鋸子通過曩昔的黃昏和黎明
此刻正在下一條街，或者更遠更深的
院子；或在水中，在電晶體的音波上

Song of Yesterday's Snow

Yesterday, descending to the pass, the snow line

(On a gloomy afternoon) came so close to me

But still it sank, and then there were white blotches in the tops

Of the dark evergreens, a sign, desire of the universe

A few remaining leaves and two winter birds perched beyond the blinds

Quiet chimneys stood smokeless

When the snow line finally descended to mid-mountain

Everyone was speeding along the freeway, sleds and skis

On roof-racks, back from the hills, so

I felt free to imagine, to speculate that it was probably because

It had already descended to six hundred feet, yesterday

As I was also free to imagine it slid on down

And the sound of river and ocean filled my ears, the wind that rose and

Fell, along with the intermittent chain saw that came from the street

    below

A chain saw? The unfinished work of autumn struggles

On in the cold, like the teeth of the T'ao-t'ie monster

The work that was not finished in summer, it

Gnaws viciously into the flesh of fallen leaves, like senses

Tracking the enticing hair in its red scarf

The sharp saw cuts through the dusk and the dawn

Just now, on the street below, or in a deep and distant

Yard; on the river, or in the sound waves of the wireless

嘩然喧喊著昨天當入冬以來第一次當
雪線終於降到山腰以下，我們有了預感
它將維持那垂沉的重力加速度，可能
就在我不自覺之間將很快滑到
山坡上那路德會教堂屋頂，然後無聲
降落，終於停在我們的窗口當我也降落

降落現在，甚至圍牆上都已經積好了
白雪，它是下來了觸及這海拔接近零
的位置。陽臺上遺留幾條猶豫的
印子現在我猜測那是一隻松鼠或
兩隻松鼠在我們不注意的時候曾經來過
並且走了。所有的出路都嚴嚴封閉了
方圓十里沒有車聲，人們在屋裏作息
幸好地下室儲備了充足的糧食和酒
他們起牀喝湯，坐在壁爐前聽氣象
洗澡上床，雪還在快樂地下著，幸好
櫃子裏有新買的避孕藥和維他命C
雪還在快樂地下，它已經低過被單
低過枕頭之類的山巒和谷壑
比我們的肩膀還低——在快樂地下著

下著，雪可能也將在一些夢中堆高
自從昨天它在我完整的意識裏

Screaming yesterday when for the first time since the beginning
    of winter
The snow line finally descended below mid-mountain, we had
    a premonition
It falls at thirty-two feet per second, perhaps
Just when I am unaware it will slide quickly down
To the roof of the Lutheran church, and afterward soundlessly
Fall, finally resting on our window as I also fall

Falling into now, even the fence around the yard piles with
Snow, it comes down to touch this place that lies nearly at
Sea level. On the balcony there are faint
Tracks that I would guess are those of a squirrel
Or two who came when I wasn't paying attention
And now are gone. All the roads out are closed
For ten miles around not the sound of a car, everyone is inside getting by
Fortunately the cellar has ample stores of food and wine
They rise, drink soup, sit in front of the fireplace listening to the weather
Take a bath, go to bed, the snow still happily falling, fortunately
There are birth control pills and vitamin C in the cabinet
The snow still happily falls, it is already below the sheets
Below the pillowy hills and valleys
Lower than our shoulders—still falling

Falling, the snow will perhaps pile high in our dreams
Since yesterday it has filled my consciousness

以快樂的型態籠罩了我們的精神
並且主動證明即使它覆滿了
各種紡織物的山巒和谷壑，它也是柔軟
和我們的肉身一樣保持著恆常的體溫
所以我這樣隨意想像，當它剛剛觸及
遠方的針葉林，我可以聽見血液
洶湧的聲音，愛和美的氣息以及
一把明快的電鋸斷續自下一條街
大聲傳來——未完成的秋天奏鳴曲
當我深入這山巒和谷壑的地帶，高過雪線
那旋律彷彿是我們期待的新歌的主題
將針葉林殺戮摧毀：宇宙之慾

一九八五·一

Blanketing our spirit with its happiness

And also actively proving that even if it covers up

All the fabric hills and valleys, still it is soft

And preserves a constant temperature like our naked bodies

Therefore I am free to imagine this, when it has touched

The evergreens far away, I can hear the sound of blood

Rushing, the breath of love and beauty as well as

The sharp scream of a saw coming intermittently

From the street below—autumn's unfinished sonata

When I slip deep into the hills and valleys, above the snow line

That melody seems to be the theme of our future songs

Destroying the evergreens: desire of the universe

January 1985

春　歌

那時，當殘雪紛紛從樹枝上跌落
我看到今年第一隻紅胸主教
躍過潮濕的陽臺——
像遠行歸來的良心犯
冷漠中透露堅毅表情
翅膀閃爍著南溫帶的光
他是宇宙至大論的見證
——這樣普通的值得相信的一個理論
每天都有人提到，在學前教育的
課堂上，浣衣婦人的閒話中，在
右派的講習班和左派沙龍裏
在兵士的恐懼以及期待
在情婦不斷重複的夢；是在
也是無所不在的宇宙至大論，他說
在地球的每一個角落每一分鐘
都有人反覆提起引述。總之
春天已經到來

他現在停止在我的山松盆景前
左右張望。屋頂上的殘雪
急速融解，並且大量向花牀傾瀉——
「比宇宙還大的可能說不定
是我的一顆心吧，」我挑戰地
注視那紅胸主教的短喙，敦厚，木訥

Spring Song

Just then, as the last of the snow was falling from the branches

I saw the first robin of the year

Hopping across the wet balcony—

As if he were a political exile returned from abroad

Tenacity showing in his cool regard

Wings glittering with the tropical sun

He is witness to the theory of the ultimate universe—

A theory so common and believable

People mention it every day, in preschool

Classrooms, in the conversations of washerwomen, in

Right-wing study groups, in the salons of the left

In the fear and expectation of soldiers

In the ever-repeating dreams of mistresses; it's there

The omnipresent theory of the ultimate universe

He says that someone cites it, someone quotes it

In every corner of the world, every minute of the day. In sum,

Spring has come

He has now stopped in front of the bonsai pine

Peering left and right. The last of the snow on the roof

Melts rapidly, pouring in torrents into the flower bed—

"Perhaps my heart just might be greater

Than the universe," in challenge

I glare at his short beak, eager and speechless

他的羽毛因為南方長久的飛拂而刷亮
是這尷尬的季節裏
最可信賴的光明：「否則
你旅途中憑藉了甚麼嚮導？」

「我憑藉愛，」他說
忽然把這交談的層次提高
鼓動發光的翅膀，跳到去秋種植的
並熬忍過嚴冬且未曾死去的叢菊當中
「憑藉著愛的力量，一個普通的
觀念，一種實踐。愛是我們的嚮導」
他站在綠葉和斑斑點苔的溪石中間
抽象，遙遠，如一滴淚
在迅速轉暖的空氣裏飽滿地顫動
「愛是心的神明……」何況
春天已經來到

一九八五‧三

His feathers polished from extended flapping in southern reaches

In a season of dumb indecision

They are the most reliable light: "Otherwise

What would guide you during your travels?"

"I rely on love," he says

Suddenly raising the level of the discussion

Beating his glittering wings, jumping into the clump of chrysanthemums

That were planted last fall and have managed to live through the harsh
　　winter

"Relying on the strength of love is a common

Concept, a type of praxis. Love is our guide"

He stands among the green leaves and the moss-speckled stones

Abstract, distant, like a teardrop

In the rapidly warming air, he shakes himself plump

"Love is the goddess of the heart . . . " How much more so

Now that spring has come

March 1985

有人問我公理和正義的問題

有人問我公理和正義的問題
寫在一封縝密工整的信上，從
外縣市一小鎮寄出，署了
真實姓名和身份證號碼
年齡（窗外在下雨，點滴芭蕉葉
和圍牆上的碎玻璃），籍貫，職業
（院子裏堆積許多枯樹枝
一隻黑鳥在撲翅）。他顯然歷經
苦思不得答案，關於這麼重要的
一個問題。他是善於思維的，
文字也簡潔有力，結構圓融
書法得體（烏雲向遠天飛）
晨昏練過玄秘塔大字，在小學時代
家在漁港後街擁擠的眷村裏
大半時間和母親在一起；他羞澀
敏感，學了一口臺灣國語沒關係
常常登高瞭望海上的船隻
看白雲，就這樣把皮膚晒黑了
單薄的胸膛裏栽培著小小
孤獨的心，他這樣懇切寫道：
早熟脆弱如一顆二十世紀梨

Someone Asked Me about Truth and Justice

Someone asked me about truth and justice

In a letter written with precise penmanship, from

A small town in another county, signed with

His real name and ID number

His age (the rain falls outside the window, dripping onto the plantain

    leaves

Onto the broken glass jagged along the top of the wall), ancestral home,

    and employment

(On the pile of dead branches in the yard

A blackbird flaps its wings.) He obviously has put a great

Deal of thought into this and still has no answer for such an important

Question. He is skilled at expressing his ideas

His characters are simple but powerful, structurally well formed

A calligraphy with style (inky clouds stream across the sky)

The Mysterious Pagoda script was his constant model, in grade school

His family lived in crowded government housing up from a fishing harbor

He spent most of the time with his mother; he was shy

And sensitive, it didn't matter that he spoke with a Taiwanese accent

His skin was tanned from going out

To gaze at the boats out at sea, to gaze at the clouds

His sunken chest protected a small

Lonely heart, he wrote so sincerely:

Maturing early, fragile as the new hybrid pear called "Twentieth Century"

有人問我公理和正義的問題
對著一壺苦茶，我設法去理解
如何以抽象的觀念分化他那許多鑿鑿的
證據，也許我應該先否定他的出發點
攻擊他的心態，批評他收集資料
的方法錯誤，以反證削弱其語氣
指他所陳一切這一切無非偏見
不值得有識之士的反駁。我聽到
窗外的雨聲愈來愈急
水勢從屋頂匆匆瀉下，灌滿房子周圍的
陽溝。唉到底甚麼是二十世紀梨呀——
他們在海島的高山地帶尋到
相當於華北平原的氣候了，肥沃豐隆的
處女地，乃迂迴引進一種鄉愁慰藉的
種子埋下，發芽，長高
開花結成這果，這名不見經傳的水果
可憐憫的形狀，色澤，和氣味
營養價值不明，除了
維他命C，甚至完全不象徵甚麼
除了一顆猶豫的屬於他自己的心

有人問我公理和正義的問題
這些不需要象徵——這些
是現實就應該當做現實處理
發信的是一個善於思維分析的人
讀了一年企管轉法律，畢業後

Someone asked me about truth and justice

Over a cup of strong tea, I sought a way to understand

How to undermine his ample evidence with abstract

Thinking, perhaps I should deny his point of departure

Attack his basic assumptions, criticize the way he has collected

His source materials, offer counterevidence to weaken his argument

Point out that everything he offers is prejudiced

Not worthy of refutation by a man of learning. Outside the window

I hear the rain falling harder

The water gushes off the roof in streams, filling the ditches all around

The house. What, after all, is this new hybrid pear—

High in the mountains on this coastal island they found

A climate similar to that of the north China plain, fertile and rich

Virgin land, to which they introduced seeds of consolation

Nostalgia, planted, sprouting and maturing

Fruit from white blossoms, a name not found in old books

Pitiful in shape, hue, and aroma

Its nutritional value unclear, except for

Vitamin C, it symbolizes nothing

Except his weak heart

Someone asked me about truth and justice

They don't need to symbolize anything—they

Are reality and one's understanding ought to be based on reality

The one who wrote the letter is skilled in thought and analysis

He studied one year of business administration and then switched to law,

半年補充兵，考了兩次司法官……
雨停了
我對他的身世，他的憤怒
他的詰難和控訴都不能理解
雖然我曾設法，對著一壺苦茶
設法理解。我相信他不是爲考試
而憤怒，因爲這不在他的舉證裏
他談的是些高層次的問題，簡潔有力
段落分明，歸納爲令人茫然的一系列
質疑。太陽從芭蕉樹後注入草地
在枝枝上閃著光。這些不會是
虛假的，在有限的溫暖裏
堅持一團龐大的寒氣

有人問我一個問題，關於
公理和正義。他是班上穿著
最整齊的孩子，雖然母親在城裏
幫傭洗衣——哦母親在他印象中
總是白皙的微笑著，縱使臉上
掛著淚；她雙手永遠是柔軟的
乾淨的，燈下爲他慢慢修鉛筆
他說他不太記得了是一個溽熱的夜
好像鬚髯父親在一場大吵鬧後
（充滿鄉音的激情的言語，連他
單挑籍貫香火的兒子，都不完全懂）

Graduated, was deferred from military service, took the law boards,

> twice . . .

The rain has stopped

His life story, his anger

His sharp questions and his accusations, I cannot understand them

Although I have sought a way to understand

Over a cup of strong tea. I don't believe it is because of the law boards

That he is so angry, since he never mentions them in his examples

The questions he asks are sophisticated, simple but powerful

His argument clearly delineated, his summary is a series of

> thought-provoking

Questions that puts everything in doubt. From behind the plantain leaves

The sun soaks into the lawn, shimmers on the dead branches. This is not

A sham, in the limited warmth

A great pocket of cold air is held firm

Someone asked me a question about

Truth and justice. He was the neatest dressed

In his class, although his mother washed clothes

For people in the city—the mother of his memory

Was fair skinned, always smiling even if there were

Tears on her face; her hands were forever soft and

Clean, in the lamplight she carefully sharpened his pencils

He said that he could not remember clearly that humid summer night

His father, perhaps after an argument

(Heated words full of localisms, not one of which even his

Only begotten son, the bearer of his family name, could understand)

似乎就這樣走了，可能大概也許上了山
在高亢的華北氣候裏開墾，栽培
一種新引進的水果，二十世紀梨
秋風的夜晚，母親教他唱日本童謠
桃太郎遠征魔鬼島，半醒半睡
看她剪刀針線把舊軍服拆開
修改成一條夾褲一件小棉襖
信紙上沾了兩片水漬，想是他的淚
如牆腳巨大的雨霉，我向外望
天地也哭過，爲一個重要的
超越季節和方向的問題，哭過
復以虛假的陽光掩飾窘態

有人問我一個問題，關於
公理和正義。簷下倒掛著一隻
詭異的蜘蛛，在虛假的陽光裏
翻轉反覆，結網。許久許久
我還看到冬天的蚊蚋圍著紗門下
一個塑膠水桶在飛，如烏雲
我許久未曾聽過那麼明朗詳盡的
陳述了，他在無情地解剖著自己：
籍貫教我走到任何地方都帶著一份
與生俱來的鄉愁，他說，像我的胎記
然而胎記襲自母親我必須
承認它和那個無關。他時常
站在海岸瞭望，據說烟波盡頭

Seems to have left, possibly perhaps he might have gone to the

   mountains

With the climate of the north China plain to open land, to raise

A newly introduced fruit, the hybrid pear, the "Twentieth Century"

On a windy fall evening she taught him a children's song in Japanese

"Momo Taro and the Island of Monsters" half asleep

He saw her cut up the old army uniform

To make a pair of lined pants and a small padded jacket

On the letter there are water stains, perhaps tears

Like mildew spreading on the wall; I look out

The sky has wept, wept for a problem

That transcends time and place

Again empty sunlight glosses over his anguished face

Someone asked me a question about

Truth and justice. From the eaves

A strange spider hangs in the false sunlight

Spinning round, weaving its web. I have watched

Mosquitoes fly in circles round

The plastic pail by the screen door, like dark, winter clouds

It's been so long since I heard such a clear and detailed

Statement, he analyzes himself:

My ancestral home would have me lug this inherited nostalgia with me

Wherever I go, he says, like a birthmark

But my birthmark is from my mother, I must

Recognize that these are quite unrelated. He

Stands on the shore gazing out, it is said that beyond the mist and waves

還有一個更長的海岸，高山森林巨川
母親沒看過的地方才是我們的故鄉
在大學裏必修現代史，背熟一本
標準答案；選修語言社會學
高分過了勞工法，監獄學，法制史
重修體育和憲法。他善於舉例
作證，能推論，會歸納。我從來
沒有收到過這樣一封充滿體驗和幻想
於冷肅尖銳的語氣中流露狂熱和絕望
徹底把狂熱和絕望完全平衡的信
禮貌地，問我公理和正義的問題

有人問我公理和正義的問題
寫在一封不容增刪的信裏
我看到淚水的印子擴大如乾涸的湖泊
濡沫死去的魚族在暗晦的角落
留下些許枯骨和白刺，我彷彿也
看到血在他成長的知識判斷裏
濺開，像炮火中從困頓的孤堡
放出的軍鴿，繫著疲乏頑抗者
最渺茫的希望，衝開窒息的硝烟
鼓翼升到燒焦的黃楊樹梢
敏捷地迴轉，對準增防的營盤刺飛
卻在高速中撞上一顆無意的流彈
粉碎於交擊的喧囂，讓毛骨和鮮血

There is another shore longer yet, high mountains, forests, and major
    rivers
Mother has never seen it, but still our hometown is there
In college, modern history was required, he memorized a book
Of answers; linguistics and sociology were electives
Good grades in labor relations, penology, and history of law
Had to make up PE and civics. He is skilled at offering examples
Giving proofs, able to argue logically, and to summarize. I have never
Received a letter so full of experience and fantasy,
Where passion and desire flow from such a deadly serious tone
So that in the end passion and desire are in equilibrium
Politely, asking me about truth and justice

Someone asked me about truth and justice
Written in a perfectly composed letter
Tear stains as wide as the dried bed of a lake
Fish frothing at the mouth die in a hidden corner
Leaving behind only a dried skeleton, blood
Seems to gush from his mature
Decisions, like a messenger pigeon in pitched battle
Released from the besieged fort, carrying the slightest hope
Of the resistance, piercing through the suffocating gunfire
Beating its wings over the tops of the scorched birch trees
It spins and swoops down toward the camp of reinforcements
But a random bullet drops it
Crumbling into the clamor of the battle, feathers, bones, and blood

充塞永遠不再的空間
讓我們從容遺忘。我體會
他沙啞的聲調，他曾經
嚎啕入荒原
狂呼暴風雨
計算著自己的步伐，不是先知
他不是先知，是失去嚮導的使徒——
他單薄的胸膛鼓脹如風爐
一顆心在高溫裏熔化
透明，流動，虛無

一九八四・一

Filling the disappearing space

That we so easily forget. I understand entirely

The reason for his hoarseness, he has

Yelled into the wilderness

Screamed in the storm

Marching to his own drum, he is not a prophet

But a disciple who has lost his guide—

His sunken chest beats like a bellows

His heart melting in the heat

Transparent, flowing, and empty

January 1984

VIDEO POEMS
The Poetry of Lo Ch'ing

The Childlike Mind

Absolutely speechless. (Courtesy of Lo Ch'ing)

馬鞍藤

一條條綠色的馬鞍藤
把金黃的沙灘
包裝成迷人的禮物
逗引海浪來看來拿

一片片淡淡的霧
把沙灘海浪
朦朧成迷人的詩謎
吸引人們去想去猜

Saddle Vine

The long arms of the green saddle vine

Wrap themselves around the golden sand

And offer it as a present

To entice the waves in for a visit

The wisps of dancing mist

Turn the waves along the beach

Into a mystifying riddle in rhyme

Which we come to puzzle from time to time

水稻之歌

早晨一醒，就察覺滿臉盡是露水
顆顆晶瑩透明，粒粒清涼爽身

回頭看看住在隔壁的大白菜
肥肥胖胖相偎相依，一家子好夢正甜

而遠處的溪水，卻是一群剛出門的小牧童
推擠跳鬧，趕著小魚，吵醒了一座矮矮短短的獨木橋

於是，我們便興高采烈的前後看齊
學著那剛登上山頂司令臺的老太陽

搖搖擺擺，把腳尖並攏
綠綠油油，把手臂高舉

迎著和風
迎著第一聲鳥鳴

成體操隊形
散——開

一散，就是
千里！

六二・五

The Rice Song

Up early in the morning, faces covered with dew
Each bead crystalline and clear, each drop comforting and cool

We turn to the cabbages that live across the fence
Healthy and plump they snuggle and cuddle, a family in sweet dreams

Water from the far creek, a passel of farm boys pouring out their doors,
Pushing and shoving, raising Cain, chasing fish, waking up the footbridge

Overflowing with excitement, back and front, right face!
Receiving instructions from the sun who climbs the mountain podium

Wafting and waving, we stand toe to toe
Green and lush, we raise our hands

Facing the sweet wind
Facing the bird's first call

We form lines at arm's length
From   each   other

For a
Thousand miles

May 1973

法相奇怪集

楔子

法相出奇怪
無非你我他

苦讀尊者

不知是那書裏無文
還是我眼中無字
還是那書中無我
還是我心中無書
還是那書本不存在
還是這我早已消失

天地之間

只剩下頑石一塊
紋路複雜的靜立一旁
默默無語

苦思尊者

莫名其妙
不知從哪裏橫飛過來
一塊火燙的大石頭
一堆難解的怪問題
如此沉重，落入雙手
十分無理，撞進心中

Bizarre Manifestations of the Dharma

The Wedge

Dharma manifestations emerge from the bizarre
Nothing more than you me him and her

The Arhat of Bitter Reading

I wonder if there's no writing in the text

Or no words in my eyes

Or no me in the text

Or no text in my mind

Or if that text really exists

Or if this me has already vanished

Between heaven and earth

Only one dumb rock remains

Intricately patterned standing quietly by itself

Silent without a word

The Arhat of Bitter Thought

How confusing

I wonder whence came flying

This big burning rock

A heap of weird indecipherable questions

As weighty as this, to fall into my arms

Totally without reason, colliding in my mind

217   Lo Ch'ing / *The Childlike Mind*

害得我站在這裏

又呆又愣
汗出如銅汁
舌卷如枯葉
差一點變成了一堆
乾渴欲裂的
碎石頭

莫思尊者

『請坐，請坐
請靜靜坐在花瓶前
學習瓶中的水
請不要思，不要想

如果心思一動，念頭一轉
那花瓶上畫的鳥
便會回過頭來
看你』

一隻畫的鳥
在畫的花瓶上
看
一個畫的人
坐在畫的石頭前
如是說

Torturing me as I stand here

Dazed and foolish
With sweat dripping like bronze juice
Tongue curled like a wilted leaf
Just short of turning into a heap of
Fragmented rock
Cracked by parching thirst

The Arhat of No Thinking

"Please, have a seat
Sit at peace in front of the flower vase
Learn from the water in the vase
Don't think, don't ponder

"If your concentration flutters, or thought wavers
Then the bird painted on the vase
Will turn its head
To watch you"

A painted bird
On a painted flower vase
Watches
A painted person
Sitting in front of a painted rock
So He spoke

抛心尊者

把凡心
輕輕從指尖
拋棄

如飄落一片
紅葉
於水中

賭氣尊者

把胸中各種鬱悶之氣
用怨恨堵住
左擠右壓
壓擠成一塊塊
奇形怪狀的小石頭

然後從嘴巴裏連續吐了出來
像不停攪動的水泥車一般
吐成一座堅固無比的大石洞
把自己層層包裹起來
南面稱王

好奇尊者

不知道
哪一片葉子
是最後一片葉子

The Arhat of Abandoning the Mind

He takes his mundane mind

Lightly with the tips of his fingers

And flicks it away

Down it floats like a single

Red leaf

Into the water

The Arhat of Battling Anger

With hatred

He isolates all the smothering anger hidden inside him

Squeezing from the left pressing from the right

Squeezing pressing it into a little

Weird-shaped strange-formed pebble

And then spits these from his mouth in a string

Just like a cement truck

Spits them out to form a solid stone grotto

Layer upon layer he wraps around himself

King upon his throne

The Curious Arhat

I wonder

Which leaf

Is the very last single leaf

於是便站在這裏
把自己搖成秋風中
第一棵枯樹

害羞尊者

我堅決認為且相信
那綠籐背後
一定没有
我所想要看的東西
絕對没有

如果有一陣風突然吹來

吹開掩映的枝葉
便會發現
籐裏籐外，空無一人
只有一朵暗紅的小花
靜靜的落在那裏

還原尊者

在一棵莊嚴寶樹的觀照之下
我慢慢靜了下來
坐在嶙峋的怪石之間
開始慢慢還原成

So here I stand

In autumn's wind swaying myself into

Its first barren tree

The Shy Arhat

I know and firmly believe

That behind those green vines

There certainly is not

Anything I would want to see

Absolutely not

If a gust of wind suddenly were to blow

Blow back those concealing branches and leaves

Then we would discover

Inside and out of those vines, not a soul

Just a cluster of small red flowers

Lying there at peace

The Arhat of Returning to Origins

Under the gaze of the august *bodhi* tree

Slowly I settle down

Sitting amidst those weird jagged rocks

Slowly starting to return to my origins—

一片平淡無奇的山壁
一任青苔野籐
爬個滿身滿臉

七○　一○、一一

Just a plain, smooth, mountain cliff

A riot of moss and wild vines

Climbing all over body and face

October and November 1981

雪夜論道

我是一幢紅色的小瓦屋
在冷冷的冬夜
向所有被冰封的道路
講解那
火紅的溫暖

七〇‧五

On the Way of Snowy Nights

I am the small cottage with a red tiled roof

In the cold, cold winter night

Explicating

The warmth of my burning fire

For all the icebound roads

May 1981

默禱記

有了電話
就可以和遠方的人
直接通話嗎？

那撥了又撥的撥號盤
盤上號碼循環，像獎券又像年代
代表著甚麼？暗示著甚麼呢
生日？誰的呀？忌日也說不定呵？
節日？出征日？結婚紀念日？
或是人人皆知又皆忘的，受難日
（也說不定都不是）

那人人進出的電話亭
像教堂又像寶塔的電話亭
展覽著甚麼？又窩藏著甚麼呀
那既非家宅旅館又非監獄病院的電話亭
說不定就是只能窩藏一名二等兵的小碉堡
說不定就是僅能展覽一個太空人的太空船
（說得定就是剛好可以收容一具屍首的薄棺材）

那翻了又翻的電話簿
那像家譜又像戶口的電話簿
難道竟會是點鬼簿不成
在電話亭裏，面對撥號盤，翻開電話簿

A Silent Prayer

Can you really

Reach out and touch someone

With a telephone?

When you dial that dial

Does the run of numbers, like a lottery ticket or an important year

Represent something, or hint at something?

A birthday perhaps, but whose? Probably not the day a loved one died

A holiday? The day of a famous battle? Or perhaps a wedding

    anniversary?

Or is it a day everybody remembers and then forgets, a day of suffering

(Or perhaps none of the above)

The phone booth where women come and go

Like a chapel, or a pagoda

What does it display, and what does it conceal?

The phone booth, not a house or hotel, not a prison or hospital

Perhaps a bunker where the infantry can hide away

Or a spaceship where astronauts are displayed

(But certainly a thin-walled coffin that easily accommodates the dead)

The phone book's dog-earred pages

Like a genealogy, like a census

Or could it be Satan's book of souls

In the phone booth, facing that dial, you open the phone book

悲哀呵，你甚至不能和你自己
和你那散逝在四方的自己，直接通話
（又何況和那遠方的人呢）

那遠在天邊的人呵
有了電話，就可以和地上的你
直接通話嗎？

六十一年一月

註：電視廣告有詞如下：

「有了電話，就可以和遠方的人通話。」

But how sad it is, you can't even reach out and touch yourself

So scattered to the four corners of the world

(To say nothing of people far away)

Could the person who is at the edge of the universe

Reach out and touch you down there on Earth

Even if he were to have a phone?

February 1972

Author's note: There is a line from a telephone company advertisement that says "With a phone you can reach out and touch someone."

請 別 看

——實 驗

…………………請別看這篇東西！其內容貧乏，無目無的，虛

聲張勢，拙劣可笑，請聽我勸！馬上扔下，幹正事去。事
實上世上的事實，早已全都擺在眼前，早已沒什麼好說了
我講的，人都做過，沒講的，人也都想過，這便是一切的
真象，聽我勸，別再看下去，後面是一團鉛黑，一片孔白
千萬別再看下去，再看，你鐵要後悔，鐵會上當，鐵定一
無所獲，唉！你看你，還是不聽——真要命——你這自以
為是的小子，你這自滿自大的傢伙，你傻瓜，你笨蛋，你
不識時務頑固難化，你……要知道，要知道以上那些時間
你都白白浪費了，就像你就像我就像古今所有的人白白浪

費自己的一生一樣，白白的浪費了浪費了浪費了…………

Don't Read This

—an experiment

...please don't read this piece! The contents are thin, without rhyme or
   reason, full of

empty promises, clumsy and absurd: You should heed my warnings. Put it
down right now, you've got more important things to do. Truthfully all
truth in this world is truly already in front of you, there is already nothing
to say about it all. What I discuss someone else has already actually done:
what I don't discuss someone else has thought of, this is the reality of the
situation, heed my warning, don't read any further; there are only black
graphite squiggles below, and empty white space. Do not under any cir-
cumstances read any further. If you go on, you will hate yourself for it, you
will be shortchanged, you will certainly get nothing in return. But, my
God, look at you, you still won't listen, what a pain you are, you self-
righteous son of a bitch, you arrogant slob, you jerk, you idiot, you don't
understand how things are, you won't change your pigheaded ways,
you... should know, should know that you have utterly misused your
time here, just as you and I, and all the people in the past have mis

used their lives, utterly misused them, utterly...

升

每一片葉子
都爲了認領及擁抱
他明年的影子
　　　　　而
　　　　　　飄
　　　　　　　落

　　　　　　　　　　　　五九・一〇

Rising

Every single leaf

In order to reclaim and embrace

Its image in the year to come

              floats

                  on

                    down

                              October 1970

毛驢小將軍
——加德滿都所見

在一條青石舖成的小巷子裏
遠遠看到一個滿頭亂髮的小孩
正使出吃奶的力氣
拼命拖一頭小毛驢

他拖了一陣子後
便伸手去扯毛驢的耳朵
扯了一陣子後
就跑去推毛驢的屁股
推了一陣了後
又改為
拉毛驢的尾巴
拉了一陣子後

乾脆！跑到附近的乾柴堆裏
抽了一根最粗的當棍子
準備朝毛驢打將過去
猛一歪頭
看到手拿相機的我
棍子突然停在半空
臉上擠出微笑一朵
空下來的那隻手

The Little Commander of Donkeys

—Katmandu

Down a narrow alley paved with dark stones

A boy with a shock of black hair

Gives his all

To get a little donkey to budge

After pulling for a bit

He yanks on its ears

And after trying that for a while

He goes around and pushes on its behind

After pushing for a bit

He tries something new

He tugs on its tail

After tugging for a while

That's it! He runs over to the woodpile there

And picks out the thickest stick

And just as he is about to smack the donkey

He turns

And sees my camera

The stick stops midair

His face breaks into a smile

And he lets fall his hand

指了指我的照相機說：
「Picture, Picture,

一個盧比，一個盧比！」
同時，立刻把棍子熟練的挾在腋下
擺了個將軍拉馬的姿勢
擺了半天，看我沒什麼反應
出人意料之外，他驟的翻身回頭
解下驢脖子上那根繩子
一溜烟——跑了

只剩下那隻小毛驢
仍然固執的站在那裏
動也不動的眨了眨眼睛
好像什麼也沒有發生的樣子

Pointing at my camera, he calls

"Une photo, une photo

One rupee, one rupee"

He thrusts the stick up under his arm

And poses there like a commander reviewing his troops

He stands for the longest time, when I don't react

He spins around

Drops the rope

And is gone in a flash

Then there is only the donkey

Still standing there, stubborn

Slowly blinking

As if nothing at all had happened

螞　　蟻

一隻螞蟻
自人海中，向你爬來
你分不清，是喜是憂
是敵？是友

螞蟻爬上鞋子
你發現你穿著的
竟是一雙戰艦——
偽裝嚴密，有如堡壘

螞蟻爬上膝蓋
你發現你光滑如大理石的身上
竟充滿了險惡——
肩是斷崖，胸是峭壁

螞蟻爬上脖子
你發現螞蟻發現了一幢茅屋
一幢有門有戶有煙囪的
簡陋小茅屋

螞蟻爬進了嘴巴
爬出了鼻孔，爬上了你的眼睛
你首次發現，螞蟻，竟是如此的
巨大，巨大——巨如恐大如龍

Ant

Out of a sea of people

An ant crawls toward you

You don't know whether to be happy or sad

Is he friend or foe?

He crawls over your shoes

And you discover that you are actually

Wearing battleships—

Camouflaged, but real fortresses

He crawls over your knee

And you discover that your smooth, marble body

Is all dangerous terrain—

Your shoulders are drop-offs, your chest a vertical wall

The ant crawls up your neck

And you discover that he discovers a thatched hut

A rustic thatched hut

With a door, chimney, and windows

He crawls into your mouth

And out of your nostril, climbing into your eye

And for the first time you discover that this ant is

Huge, dinosaurianly huge

241   Lo Ch'ing / *The Childlike Mind*

終於，螞蟻爬入了腦際
進出了夢中⋯⋯⋯⋯⋯
代你繼續編織你所有未完的夢幻
而你發現，你已不能再發現

Finally the ant crawls into your brain

In and out of your dreams

Weaving for you all your unfinished fantasies

And you discover that you are able to discover no more

星星・星・星
——起　音

昨夜，不知不覺
逝去的露水

今夜，又悄悄悄悄的
回來了

回來了
回來了

又悄悄悄悄，回到我
不知不覺的臉上來了

Stars, Stars, and More Stars

—tuning up

The dew that vanished
Last night without a trace

Has come back tonight
Like a thief

Has come back
Back

Has like a thief come back again
Unknown traces on my face

請把日光燈打開

走進教室
學生還沒有來
看看窗外，依舊是
陰時晴偶陣雨的天氣

窗子有的有打開，有的沒有
窗外的風景也隨著玻璃上
或多或少的灰塵
或明或暗

下意識的，我掏出了
衛生紙，走了過去
開始擦窗子
這才發現

有的有玻璃，有的沒有
有的透明，有的半透明
嗯，學校教室總是這樣的
我把四五十塊玻璃大致擦了一陣

四點八分
身後傳來學生進門的聲音
我轉頭看了看坐在牆角門邊的那個
閒閒的說：「請把日光燈打開。」

Fluorescent Lights

Coming into the classroom
Before the students arrive
I notice outside the window
It is cloudy and still raining lightly

Some of the windows are open, some closed
The scenery is reflected along in them
Some grimy, some not so
Some clear, some dark

Unconsciously I take a tissue
Out of my pocket and go over
And start to wipe them clean
And discover then

Some of the windows have glass in them, some don't
Some are transparent, some translucent
Classrooms here are always like this
I clean panes while I wait

At 4:08
Behind me I hear the students filing in
I turn to the one sitting in the corner by the door
And suggest, "Can we have some light in here?"

寫　生

魚兒說：
湖水最愛
靜靜對著高山
做水彩寫生

可是，剛剛畫好一張
彩色還沒乾
就被微風頑皮的小手
給弄亂了
然而，湖水卻
一點也不生氣
她只不過皺一皺眉
笑了笑
很有耐心的
重新再畫一張

嗯，畫得又快又好
我看了，高興得
翻起觔斗來
潑剌一聲——為她喝采
不料
卻又把
她的畫
給弄壞了

A Life Sketch

[a poem for children]

The fish said:

The quiet pond loves to

Do watercolor sketches of

Tall mountains

But as soon as it finishes one

And before the paint has dried

The little hand of the mischievous breeze

Comes to mess it up

Still the pond

Is not mad at all

It just wrinkles its brow

Smiles

And patiently

Begins to paint another one

This time painting better and quicker

And when I see it

I jump for joy

Creating quite a splash

Never realizing

I would ruin

Her painting

Again

Love and Death

Rather, it was to say I would love her forever.
(Courtesy of Joseph R. Allen)

報仇的手段

第一招

　　縱然
你要吃我吞我
我仍愛你戀你
　　如故

食慾之後

我會要你，慢慢學習
如何，也用愛
來消化難以消化的我
辛，辛，苦，苦
消我，成你的全部份
化你，成我的一部份

第二招

　　刀劍毀
　　　　彎弓折
怨毒的眼光，寸斷成灰
無，助，的，我
終不得不合掌闔目
和衣躺在你的，腳下
成為泥土！成為緩緩隆起的
泥，土

Means of Revenge

Strategy 1

Even if

You want to eat me, to swallow me whole

I would love you still, be devoted to you

    As before

And after dinner

I would have you slowly learn

How to digest indigestible me

With love

So painfully

Ingesting me, I become all of you

Diminishing you, you become part of me

Strategy 2

Swords and sabers destroyed

    Bows and arrows broken

And venomous looks turn to scattered ashes

I, less hope

In the end can only lie at your feet

Clothed, eyes lowered and hands in prayer

And there become mud, a slowly rising pile

Of mud

緩緩隆起的泥土
不斷緩緩隆起隆起
隆起，隆你至至高
起你至，至寒
然後，再急崩速潰
再掩你，埋你……

第三招

　　我，是你
唯一的，敵人
唯一的，刺客

滿懷仇恨的我
爲了陷你害你
總是挖空心思
想儘計謀——
那種種不同的計謀
那和你逃避的方法
一樣多的，計謀

爲了殺你
我不惜施展最毒最後的
手段——殺了我自己
因爲，這樣
你就安了心，就得了意
就不會再時時刻刻

A slowly rising pile of mud

Rises slowly

Raising you to the heights

Lifting you up into the cold

And then, in a great collapse, in a sudden slide

Smothers you, buries you . . .

Strategy 3

I am

Your only enemy

Your only assassin

Filled with revenge, I

Dredge my thoughts

Devising schemes

To entrap, to hurt you—

Schemes of all kinds

A scheme

For your every escape

To kill you

Without mercy I execute this last, most venomous

Act—I kill myself

Because this way

You'll relax, get what you want

And won't spend all your hours

不眠不休的思我
念我……

絕　　招

沒有出口，我是你腳下的路
是路上的地氈，氈中的羅網

沒有窗戶，我是你尋求庇護的房屋
空洞安全得如一靜靜埋伏的，墳墓
沒有欄杆，我是誘你憩臥的床褥
軟軟綿綿，催你長眠

然而，我卻更喜歡成為你的
貼身愛妾，潔白而嬌巧
似一柄冰涼光滑的——匕首
冰冰涼涼，光光滑滑
我，刺進你的胸膛
溫溫柔柔，殘殘忍忍
我，與你的胸膛，合而為一
一為而合，而沒人曉得

而沒人曉得——
面目猙獰的你
竟死不甘心的，拼命抓著我搯著我
漸軟漸弱漸漸無聲………
無息無力，無形無神無影
無成一個雙手緊握刀柄的

Restlessly, sleeplessly thinking of me

Remembering me

The Ultimate Strategy

With no way out, I am the road under foot

The rug on the road, the weave in the rug

With no window, I am the room where you seek refuge

Empty and safe like a tomb waiting in silent ambush

With no rail, I am a mattress seducing you into sweet dreams

Soft and cuddly, urging you on to eternal rest

Nevertheless, I would prefer to become your

Adoring mistress, pure and dainty

Like an icy, gleaming blade

So terribly cold, with such a gleam

I would pierce your breast

So terribly kind, so cruel

We would be one together

Together be one, and no one would know

And no one would know—

With your repulsive face

Defying death, you seized me, holding on for dear life, strangled me

Softening, weakening, gradually falling silent

No breath, no strength, no spirit, no shape, no shadow

Absented into a knife handle grasped in two hands

我，駭然發現
刀刃沒入的地方
竟是我自己的
胸膛

I would be shocked to discover

How the blade has now sunk

Into my own

Breast

May 1971

道

「你的愛情像椅子
誰都可以隨意坐」

他對她對　祂　對他對她……
如是說道唱道罵道嘆道笑道講
道

六五・十

The Way

"Your love is like a chair
In which anyone can take his ease"

He to her to   One   to him to her
Was the way it was said, sung, sworn, sighed, sneered, and spoken a
Way

May 1971

織錦記

丈夫病了
這是從來沒有的事………

壁鐘的長針以鐘聲尖尖刺我一下
呵，下午了，下午一點了
孩子們照常在學
汽車飛機照常駛過
電視懂事的臥在一邊，安靜蠢笨似懶豬
長篇小說俯跪在沙發上，默默禱告如女尼
日報在門旁還未打開
整個世界就靜靜卷縮在那裡

一切暫停
只有金絨線般的陽光
溫和有禮，費事的從窗口爬了進來
腳步輕得像個醫護人員
緩緩走近丈夫的床邊
順手把院中菟絲花的影子
悄悄繡在軟軟的枕頭上
細細插入厚厚的錦被裏

還是繼續去織那塊沒織完的花巾吧，一針針
把戀愛結婚，把那甜甜蜜蜜吵吵鬧鬧的往事
統統織進去吧，織進現在的憂愁焦慮未來的

Needlework

My husband

Has never been sick before . . .

The minute hand of the wall clock stabs me with its piercing chime

It's afternoon now, one o'clock in the afternoon

The children are at school as usual

Cars and planes keep going by as usual

But the TV understands, lying over there quiet and dumb like a lazy pig

The thick novel kneels on the sofa, silently praying like a nun

The newspaper is over by the door still unopened

With the whole world rolled up inside

For a moment, everything stops

There is only a ray of sunshine, a golden strand of yarn

Mildly and politely, taking the time to crawl in through the window

On footsteps as quiet as those of a nurse

As it gradually approaches my husband's bed

It secretly embroiders on his plump pillow

The shadows of the courtyard's wisteria

Slipping into the folds of his thick embroidered quilt

I might as well continue to work on that unfinished piece, stitch by stitch I

knit in love and marriage all the sweet tender angry tearful times of the

past knitting in today's worry and today's sadness along with the dreams

幻想憧憬織進去織進去把一方白色的大花巾
織成我整個下午的寂寞，把針尖複雜多變的
心情織成固定重複的圖案。呵，這精工製成
的花巾，蔽電視太大蓋沙發嫌小，做餐巾呢
又讓人覺得太過浪費——還是拿去輕輕蓋在

　　　丈夫的身上吧

可是，可是這是從來從來沒有的事吶
假如丈夫生病了的話……

六十一年十二月

and desires of the future knitting knitting them in and knitting the white patterned piece into the loneliness of my endless afternoon, knitting my thoughts with all their complicated stitches into its clear repeating patterns. Yes, it's an exquisitely done piece, too big to shroud the TV, way too small to cover the couch, if I were to use it for a tablecloth people would think it extravagant—I might as well use it

to cover my husband's body

Yet, my husband has never ever been sick before
But supposing he were . . .

December 1972

房　子

本來是坐在廊前，看下雨的
看院裏新翻的泥土，看土中
我們新栽的松苗
如今，雨一停
便頓然覺得無事可做了

你起身說，要走
我，沒作聲
你走時，我只送到大門口
大門欲言又止，張著嘴
期期艾艾的，呆想了半天
沒說什麼
一旁的我，一時
也想不出該說些什麼
至於四週冒雨趕來送行的山
喘得一頭一臉的霧水，飄飄
浮浮，連站都沒站穩
自然，就更不便再多話了

夾道的竹子都猜不透
爲何這次，你沒在橋頭駐足，回首
於是，便一夥夥的聚在一旁
沙沙沙沙的揣測了開
這一來，惹得剛要平靜下來的我

The House

Earlier, sitting here on the veranda we looked out on the rain falling

And out on the newly turned soil in the courtyard, we looked out on

The pine seedlings that we had recently planted there

But now, since the rain has stopped

Suddenly it's as if there were nothing left to do

You get up and say, it's time to go

I don't make a sound

When you leave I see you only as far as the gate

Opening its mouth, the gate almost speaks but doesn't

Stuttering, blankly staring there

Saying nothing

Off to the side, for a moment

I can't imagine what I should say either

Mountains have come from afar braving the rain to see you off

Panting, they exhale cliffs and ridges of mist and rain, floating off

Drifting up, even they can not stand steady

So naturally, I am now even more self-conscious about speaking

The bamboo that line the road cannot imagine

Why this time you didn't stop on the bridge and look back

Thus, clump by clump they gather to the side

And speculate in murmuring voices

And in this way upset me so

又十分不安起來，慢慢……
我又感到自己是一幢空洞而歪斜的房子了

我站著，寂寞的站著
胸中充滿了悲哀
在風中在林中在謠言聲中
我，不知所措的站著
一如那無人依靠的柴扉
簡直不堪吹拂

不自覺的，我掩上了大門
忽然聽見，身後有松子落下的聲音
微微一驚，我迅速回頭——發現
不知何時，剛插的松苗
竟已然成蔭了——
挺拔而青翠的，站在院中
用影子柔柔的，撫慰著我
充滿愛意的，撫著我慰著我
灑了我一臉……水珠

水珠繽紛，滾動在我的臉上
涼涼的，抬著一幅水珠的臉
我向天望去，碰巧——天
也正以一幅星星的臉，向我望來
我禁不住會心的笑了，笑裏
摻雜著幾許淒涼，幾許絕望

When I am just about calm again, but slowly . . .

And again I feel that I am a house collapsing and abandoned

I stand, stand lonely

With my heart full of grief

In the wind, in the woods, among the rumors

I stand not knowing what to do with myself

As helpless as the garden gate that no one holds

Against the blowing wind

Absentmindedly I close the gate

When the sharp sound of a pine cone falling behind me

Startles me, I turn to look and discover,

I don't know for how long it has been, that the seedlings just planted

Are already casting shade across the courtyard

Standing tall and blue-green there

They soothe and comfort me with their shade

Overflowing with lovely intentions, soothing and comforting me

Sprinkling my face with drops of water

The drops of water roll down my cheeks in streams

Cool, I raise my glistening face

To gaze toward the sky, and the sky's starry face

Happens to be gazing back at me

I can't help but laugh to myself

But that laugh is filled with such loneliness, such despair

唉，你知道嗎
當你走時，我是多麼的想和你說幾句
道別的話……
可是，可是你又哪能曉得當時
當時我的心裏，是多麼多麼的
害怕啊，我怕，我怕萬一在張口的瞬間
我真的變成了一幢空洞而歪斜的
房子，那可該怎麼辦
怎麼辦呢

But do you know

When you left, how much I wanted to say just a few words

Of parting . . .

But how could you have ever known at that time

How in my heart I was so very

Frightened, I was afraid, afraid that at the moment I opened my mouth

I just might really turn into a house

Collapsing and abandoned, then what would I do

What could I ever do?

May 1971

冤魂記

——與蒲松齡夜談

陰風向琴弦索鳴
腐葉向長廊索步
　　雲異星邪
紙窗雪白，發出磨牙之音
木門無聲，裂開微笑一縫

忽然，昏雲吞月
大地驟然一暗
暗空中，有燈籠一盞
上下飄浮，圓圓而來
燈而無影
燭而不焰
緩緩游移過
一間又一間的廂房
吹熄了房中一張又一張
張口瞪眼驚怖萬分的臉龐

然後是死寂
死寂如血……
慢慢自四壁的皮膚裏滲出
驀的，從門重疊處
拋來一絲尖細的笑聲——
拋來細髮鋼線一道

The Avenging Ghost

—talking with P'u Sung-ling

A sullen wind entices music from the lute strings

Rotten leaves scuttle toward the sheltering arcade

    Strange clouds, bizarre stars

Paper windows, white as snow, grate like grinding teeth

The wooden gate stands slightly ajar, smiling a thin, soundless grin

Suddenly, the murky clouds swallow the moon

And everywhere the earth is sunk into darkness

In this darkened emptiness a single paper lantern

Floats up and down, round and round it goes

Lamp but no shadow

Light but no flame

Leisurely it roams

Through the pavilion into one bedroom then another

Putting out the light, one by one, of the faces

Terrified, mouth-gaping, wide-eyed faces

And then it is deadly quiet

Quiet like blood . . .

Oozing slowly from the skin of the four walls

Suddenly from deep within the entryway

A thin piercing laugh rises—

Rising like a strand of fine wire

刺穿層層的幽暗
引出烈火一把，怪煙一陣

濃煙撲打樑上的積塵厚厚
灰塵手帕般摀住了吱吱做響的家具
火舌舔掃地上的積血斑斑
血滴淚水般驚醒了駭然而靜的庭院

庭院之上
圓月復現
冷冷掛在熊熊烈火之中
漠漠照在牆角陰黑之處

但見
一隻蒼白的纖指
半露在沙土外
微微一動

　　　　　　　　　　　　　　　　丙辰・夏

Puncturing the layers of dark

It draws along with it a burst of flame, a strange wind

The heavy smoke smothers the dust piled thickly on the beams

The ashes cover the creaking furniture like shrouds

Tongues of flame lick the blood-spattered ground

Like tears, drops of blood awaken the quiet, fearful courtyard

Above the courtyard wall

The round moon reemerges

Hanging there coldly among the roaring flames

Silently shining into the dark corners of the wall

And there sticking up from the dirt

A pale, emaciated finger

Beckons to you

Ever so slightly

Summer 1976

苦 肉 記

我是如此的深深愛著他
別人是不知道的……
也無法知道

我不得不殺了他
爲保存我完整無缺的愛

我替他發喪，舉祭，且宴飲
但卻没把他埋藏
我依舊讓他在人群中行走
走在細心的化粧之後
穿著入時，談笑自若
依舊戀愛、做愛、談愛
從事一切見得見不得人的事情

没人相信我就是那站在一旁微笑的
兇手，就連他也不信

因爲，他是如此徹底的殺了我
我和他，都不知道
也都不願知道

六十五年二月

Self-Sacrifice

I love her so deeply

And no one else knows . . .

How could they ever know

I just had to kill her

In order to preserve my pure, flawless love

I had a funeral for her, offered prayers, and a memorial dinner too

But I did not bury her

I let her walk, as before, among the living

After she was carefully made up, to go out

Wearing the latest fashions, chatting at her ease

As in days gone by, to be in love, to make love, to love

To carry on with all our shameful and shameless affairs

No one believes that I am her murderer standing off to the side

Smiling, not even she believes

Because she has so thoroughly killed me

Neither she nor I know

And neither of us wants to know

February 1976

遠處傳來馬達的聲音
——虎尾所聞

一隻黃狗趴在門口，看一隻水牛
一隻水牛臥在欄外，看幾隻鴨子

幾隻鴨子伸頭入水
探探藍天，找找太陽

而太陽藍天，卻高高在上
垂罩一切，籠照一切

籠罩著無人的菜園，長草的水田
安靜的廚房，破敗的神案

垂照著城外墳堆中的阿傳嫂
城內人堆中的兒孫們

更仔細照在鴨子水牛黃狗
照在一張頭戴斗笠剛要下田的臉上

呵，凡此種種，一切安祥，安祥和平而無人知曉
在阿傳伯死後，第七天的早上

63 · 1

The Sound of a Motor Coming from Afar

—heard in the hamlet of Wu-wei

An old dog collapsed in the doorway watches a cow

Who sleeps outside her pen watching some ducks

The ducks dunk their heads

Searching for the blue sky, looking for the sun

But the sun and sky are high above

A cover over everything, shining on everything

Shining over the neglected garden, the paddy that stands in weeds

The quiet kitchen and the dilapidated family shrine

Shining on Auntie Ch'uan among the tombs outside the city

And on her children among the crowds in the city

Shining even more on the ducks, cow, and dog

Shining on the face of someone in a straw hat going out into the fields

And each so tranquil, so tranquil no one knows it is

The morning of the seventh day after the death of Uncle Ch'uan

January 1974

279   Lo Ch'ing / *Love and Death*

苦茶記

「茶苦原來即苦茶」
　　——沈兼士：「又和一首自調」

到處找你，都不在
許是雪深，掩埋了你的足跡

初次看你
你說：坐坐坐坐
抬頭看你
你說：喝茶喝茶
回頭看你
你說：去去就來

我細撫石桌的殘舊
看茶由淡轉濃轉澀轉苦
轉而使枯萎的茶花轉香轉開轉盛
如盛開的雪花，佈滿了我來你去的艱險路上
我緊握熱茶，讓溫暖
緩緩遍佈全身

四周漸暗漸冷，你愈去愈久
寂寞裏，我以粗笨的手，沾漸涼的茶
在堅冷的石上，寫透明的「愛」
默默，我看見這充滿清純苦澀的「愛」

Bitter Tea

"Life's bitterness comes from bitter tea"
  —Shen Chien-shih

I looked for you everywhere, but you were never there

Perhaps the heavy snows covered your tracks

When I first saw you

You said, "Come on in, sit down"

As I raised my gaze to you

You said, "Have some tea"

And when I looked again

You said, "I'll be right back"

I run my hand over the rough stone table

Watching the weak tea turn strong, then sour, then bitter

Turning so, its dried blossoms turn fragrant, then fresh, then lush

Fresh and lush as the heavy snow that covers the perilous road by

    which I came and by which you left

I hold onto the hot tea, letting its warmth

Seep slowly into my body

All around it grows cold and dark, and you are gone longer and longer

In my loneliness I dip a thick finger into the tea that has grown cool

And on the cold, hard stone write a transparent "love"

Silently I watch that "love" filled with purity and bitterness

在熾熱的指劃中，不斷消失揮發
化入周圍黑冷的空氣之中

然後，再寫一個
再寫一個……
每個愛字，寫法不同
消失揮發的也不同
而茶水始終盈盈
而你，始終不見回來

也許，你早已回來
也許，你根本没去
也許，你就在我身邊
而我既没察覺也没想到
我一直没察覺想到，你
也許一直就在我的手中：

一杯漸涼的茶
使黑冷中的我，沸騰

六十年七月

From the stroke of my burning finger swiftly vanish as it evaporates

Into the black, cold air that surrounds me

And then, I write it again

And again . . .

Each time the character "love" is written differently

And each time it evaporates differently

But the tea is never diminished

And you never come back

Perhaps you already have come back

Perhaps you never even left

Perhaps you are here at my side

But I have never realized, never imagined

I never ever realized, or imagined, you were

Perhaps always in the palm of my hand:

A cup of tepid tea brings me

In the darkening cold to a boil

July 1971

天　仇　報

‧‧‧更敲三下
一個箭步，我率領冷風一陣
翻上你裏外重疊的高牆
俯查你鈎心鬥角的屋宇

且趁機混入片片初降的白雪
無聲無息，飄入你陰森險惡的院落
隱入你手植纖弱的竹叢，成爲你荷槍欲睡的警衛
我——是來暗殺你的

雪呵！密祕伏伺在五彩的玻璃瓦上
瓦下，有你溫香軟玉的臥床
血呵！密密凝結在冷僻的亂葬崗上
崗下，有我失散多年的父母

嘿，你想仔細聽聽那雪落的聲音嗎
那就聽我緩緩向你的步履吧
我的步履安靜，靜如我的影子，而我的影子
正肆無忌憚，四處碰撞你價值連城的古玩

喏喏，現在我碰到的，正是你愛之若命的細腰花瓶
就讓空洞冷涼的她，保護我隱藏我而背叛你吧

Heaven's Revenge

...the third watch begins and

With a lunge that stirs a gust of wind

I leap over your walls, outer then inner

To peer down into your intricately designed rooms

Seizing the chance I merge with the flakes of falling snow

And float down soundlessly into your shadowed, forbidding courtyard

I hide among the wispy bamboo that you planted with your own hand,

becoming your bodyguard, rifle shouldered in a near doze

It is I—come to murder you

Snow. Lying in secret ambush on the multicolored roof tiles

Below the tiles, your warm, delicate bed

Blood. Thickly congealed on the cold hill of unmarked graves

Below the hill, my long lost parents

If you would like to listen closely to the sound of the falling snow

Then listen to my footsteps coming slowly toward you

My footsteps are quiet, quiet as my shadow, and my shadow

Fearless and carefree, keeps bumping into your high-priced antiques

Just now I bumped into that narrow-necked vase that you treasure

more than life itself

I'll let her, since she is so cold and vacant, protect me, conceal me,

rebelling against you

你想夢見那瓶外的落花和種子的去向嗎
那就夢見我吧

你夢中的我
和你的臥房心房一樣
是無比幽暗的
我眼前的你
和我的眼睛尖刀一般
是閃閃發光的

配合著你濕熱均勻的呼吸
我把筆直閃亮的利刃——刺入你柔軟起伏的胸膛
刹那間，這周圍…………呵，這整個宇宙的寂靜
是多麼的美妙誘人呀

If you want to dream about the petals and seeds that have fallen

from that vase

Then dream about me

The me of your dreams

Along with your heart and your bedroom are alike

Blacker than the night

The you caught in the gaze of my eyes

Along with my eyes and my dagger are alike

Flashing with light

In rhythm with your warm, moist, steady breathing

I raise the sharp, thin, gleaming blade—and drive it into your softly

rising, falling chest

For an instant, everything around . . . with the universe caught in silence

Is so alluring and beautiful

劫後英雄吟

喂，老兄
你怎麼不聲不響
靠在樹後——嚇我一跳
………眞是的

怎麼？受了委屈還是犯了錯
唉唉，只不過是受點騙罷了
没啥了不起，大家都一樣的
還是快快回家去吧

嘿，老兄
年紀不小啦，怎麼還亂使小性子
怎麼還懷著那把破銹稀爛的
三八步槍，死命對著我

快別他媽的開玩笑了，雪花早已溶化
冬天……春天是是非非的也都快過了
咱倆既没前嫌又無新仇，難道到現在你還想
還想在我胸前插他奶奶的一朵血花去報功不成

Heroes in the Aftermath

Hey, man

What are you doing there, not making a sound

Hiding behind that tree, scaring me half to death

. . . You're really something

What is it? Someone do you wrong or have you really screwed up

this time

No, there's just a little scam going down, that's all

It's nothing special, its the same with everybody

Lct's just get on home now

Y'know, brother

You're a grown boy, how come you're still acting like a kid

How come you're still holding that rusty, broken-down

M-1 on me, why are you so deadly serious

Quit making those fucking jokes, the snow's already melted

Winter . . . even spring, right or wrong, will soon be gone

You and me, we had no beef before, nothing's changed,

how come you still want

Want to be a hero and stick that mother-fucking bloody corsage

on my chest

哈，老弟，你怎麼老是娘娘腔腔的
頭不抬嘴不張，賴在那根禿禿的樹幹上
連那樣老大的太陽，在樹間用頭頂在雲間用手搖
都搖你頂你不醒，你到底是裝那門子睡呀

呵，老弟呀老弟
要睡就睡到我身旁來吧
雖然我們連路人也談不上
雖然我們竟因此成了敵人
但看到你我散掛在樹枝上下那幅開肉舖的樣子
大家還敵個屁嘞

呸！滾他娘的服裝整齊儀容莊嚴左轉右轉立正稍息
十月一到，你看吧，我包準那紅葉黃葉又會齊集在我倆身上
配合著落日落月，向我們獻上幾滴紅露燒酒
那酒啊，可真他妹子的涼死人哦

Hey, man, how come you're such a sissy

You won't lift your eyes, won't open your mouth

Even the sun, butting its head against the trees, shaking its hand

in the clouds

Can't shake or pound you awake, what's this sleep you're up to now

Well, brother

If you want to sleep, come sleep here beside me

Although we don't know each other as well as passersby

Although this thing has made us each other's enemy

But look, you and I hang here in these branches like meat at

the butchery

It's those assholes who are enemies, not us

Shit, to hell with those mother-fucking uniforms, serious looks,

left face, right face, attention, at ease

Look, November's here, I tell you all those red and yellow leaves will

fall and cover our bodies, you and me

With the setting sun and setting moon, a few drops of Mad Dog

That booze can really fucking freeze you to death

Ars Poetica

And obediently the palm trees stand in line waiting for the cross-town bus. (Courtesy of Lo Ch'ing)

不瞞您說

瞞過父母

瞞不過碗筷

瞞過碗筷

瞞不過衣帶

衣帶帶衣

在風中飛舞

在飛中舞字

舞出我心中想的那個

藍如青天綠如春天紅如

臉紅的，那個字

六五・八

Not to Keep Anything from You

Having kept it from Mother and Father,

You cannot keep it from the forks and spoons

Having kept it from the forks and spoons

You cannot keep it from the belt of your pants

Pants' belt belting pants

Flying in the wind's dance

The words dance in the wind

From deep within my deepest thoughts that

Are as blue as the sky, as green as spring, as red as

A blush, the word

August 1976

詠風季

西南季風善書
善飛白書

東海之波記云：
運時間爲墨，汲月光爲水
研日盤爲硯，集電閃爲毫
展青青晴空爲長長的手卷
展無邊的草原
展——海

見孤鳥出入亂林
乃悟筆法

方一出鋒——
即有墨雲捲雪之勢
魚龍暗驚，泉石驟醒
筆力所及——
群葉慌慌向四處聚散奔逃
且走且戰八方伏躍之龍嶺

一點一啄，儘成空谷
一挑一趯，皆開山洪

怒時，似勁雨追地
緩時，若春草漫發

Ode to the Southwest Wind

In the spring the southwest wind has a fine hand
Especially fine in brushstrokes of air and light

The waves of the East China Sea offer testimony:
Putting time in motion for its ink, dipping into moonlight for water
The face of the sun is its inkstone, flashes of lightning its brush
Unrolling long handscrolls of blue sky
Of limitless grasslands, and unrolling
The sea

After you have seen a lone bird fly in and out of the deep woods
Then you really understand calligraphy

The tip of its brush strikes—
It is filled with inky clouds and snowy splashes
In the depths dragons are startled, stones suddenly awakened
The power of the brush moves—
Autumn leaves pile up and scatter across the world, blown on
Running and fighting over the undulating ridges that fill the sky

A dot and a dash form a lonely valley
A hook and stroke set off mountain floods

Agitated it looks like sheets of rain across the ground
Relaxed it resembles the sweet growth of spring grasses

頹，則如稻黍垂頹之深深
每每意落北海之初，而心已收東南之末
隨手間，寫下江河
如寫下一幅豪情萬里的狂草對聯

或藏斧斤於垂露之內
或示利刃於流星之外

或開懷納霧
或收合煙霞
依與之所至
時而肘縱，時而管奔
常放雲牧雨
略星空以西之西而去

而九月
評曰：

如嚐榛莽之辛辣
品凍原之極寒
木葉落定
而波濤落平之後
其書味之深——
與海深，齊

Leaning over like grain collapsing under full and heavy ears

Each intention starts out from the northern sea, thoughts gather

    together in the southwest reaches

And nonchalantly it writes the two rivers

Writes them into a long crazy cursive couplet full of feeling

It might either conceal an ax head in the light dew

Or express a sharp blade beyond the shooting stars

It might either welcome the fog with open arms

Or bring together the mist and clouds

According to its inner desires

Sometimes the elbow flies, or the stylus runs

Releasing the clouds and setting off the rain

Occupying the west of west in the starry sky, it departs

But September

Offers this final evaluation:

It is like a taste of entangled misfortune

A brush with the arctic cold

After the leaves have fallen

And the waves flattened out

The depth of its calligraphic style

Is as the sea, deep

November 1969

臨池偶得

自墨綠墨綠的池底
佳句如紅魚
悄悄悄悄的
浮現

忽的轉身

又靜靜沉入我
幽深的心底

六九・四

Found by the Pool

From the bottom of the dark green pool

Clever phrases like goldfish

Float silently

Silently into sight

Turn suddenly

And sink quietly into the

Hidden depths of my mind

April 1980

黑 之 子

一日苦樂之後
一場敵友之後
又到我一人
面對棋坪的時間了

垂眉靜坐如清茶沉澱百慮
細細衡量似香菸神思飛昇
打昨日未完的劫
下今日未下的子

手臂歪斜支住歪斜的頭顱
頭顱歪斜撐住——
從整個天宇上斜傾下來的黑夜
在這最深最暗的時刻

於是，有人開始在暗地裏
以風雲的詭譎把局佈下
佈下一些似星似鑽似燭似淚的玩意
一些忽隱忽現忽東忽西的白子

仰首看了看
我那多年來唯一的對手：
狡詐萬分的朋友，無微不至的敵人
低頭握了握，掌中堅實圓潤的黑子

The Game of Go, Black Pieces

After a day of ups and downs
After a session with friend and foe
It's time for me
To face the board again

Eyes lowered in meditation, like green tea, precipitating strategies
With due care, my evaluations like incense smoke, thoughts arising
I carry through with yesterday's unfinishcd sequences
And today set in position the pieces yet to be used

My slanting arm supports my slanting skull
And my slanting skull
Holds up the black night that slants down from the heavens above
At this deepest and darkest moment

Thereupon, someone begins in the dark
To arrange his opening in strange variations of wind-blown clouds
Like stars and diamonds, candles and tears, to arrange those playthings
Those white pieces suddenly here, then gone; suddenly right, then left

Raising my head I look at
My sole opponent of these many years:
My infinitely slimy friend, my totally sympathetic enemy
Head lowered, I fondle the hard, black pieces, glossy in my palm

我是一個
在空虛中
在智慧愚昧不到處
佈局落子的人

佈局是我的長考
長考是我的熟睡
熟睡是我的夢想
夢想是我的醒來

哦，我將不斷的熟睡長考夢想醒來
握著手中跳動不安的黑子，在對手的眼中
旭日般，以一種天地萬物重新定位的方式
醒來

六五·一

I am

In the void

In the place where intelligence and ignorance never reach

Arranging sequences, setting down pieces

Sequences are my deliberations

Deliberation is my sleep

Sleep is my dream

The dream is my awakening

Yes, I shall go on sleeping, deliberating, dreaming, waking

Holding in my hand the restless black pieces, in my opponent's eyes

Like the morning sun, with new positions set for the earth, sky,

    and all the creatures

I awaken

January 1976

養雲齋讀畫記
——致野遺生龔賢

我家掛了幅龔半千
現在你一定看不見
照你站的位置，至多只能看到
我家門前的五棵柳樹
柳樹下的清水草塘
塘草中的木蘭扁舟
還有那蘭舟旁
大大小小蠢蠢欲動的花青石頭

那些石頭，原是一堆瞎吵胡鬧的癩蛤蟆
只因冒犯下凡夜浴的星星
統統被罰變成了啞巴
默默照顧成群青草化身的游魚
至於岸邊的柳樹
有四棵正想彎下身來玩水
卻被另一棵斜斜打橫攔住——
像是在勸他們
不要吵醒那剛剛睡著的小蘭舟

蘭舟柳葉般依在池塘的頰旁
池塘媽媽般擁抱滿懷的雲堆

Reading Paintings
in the Cloud-Nourishing Studio

For Kung Hsien

In my house hangs a Kung Hsien

But there is no seeing it

From where you stand, at most you might see

The five willows by my front door

The grassy pool beneath the willows

The magnolia sampan in the pool

And beside the boat

Indigo rocks, large and small, itching to make trouble

Those rocks were actually once a pond of croaking frogs

Who affronted the stars during their evening bath

And were condemned to be deaf-mutes

Now in silence they watch schools of fish with grassy shapes

Among the willows on the bank

Four bend down to splash in the water

But the other one leans across to block their reach—

As if to warn them

Not to wake the sampan that has just fallen asleep

Like a willow leaf the magnolia boat clings to the pool's cheek

And the pool bundles clouds to its breast motherlike

哦！那白鵝似的白雲堆
都是我家後院水井飼養的
他們互枕互依推推擠擠
正在睡濃濃的午覺
其實，白雲的懷裏也有個睡懶覺的
那是我的老鄰居，富春山

富春山對我家最清楚了，因為
我的東西南北窗一年四季都是大開的
你甚至在一里外，就可以聞到我桌上的酒杯，杯中的菊花
然你就偏偏看不見我掛的那幅龔半千
無論站在哪個位置哪個角度
你甚至連我也看不見
因為，我可能是桌底那個愛說話的大酒甕
也可能是那尊在雲中夢見你的富春山
更可能是把你畫入畫中的，龔半千

六十三年一月

Those swan clouds

Are nourished by the well in my backyard

They push and crowd, leaning and pillowing on each other

During their long afternoon nap

And actually there is someone else who oversleeps in their embrace

My old neighbor, Mount Fu-ch'un

Mount Fu-ch'un knows all about my house, since

The windows stand open through the seasons, north, south, east, and
    west

You can smell the wine that stands on my table from a mile away, and
    the chrysanthemums in the wine too

But you can never ever see the Kung Hsien that hangs in my house

No matter your position, no matter the angle

You can't even see me

Perhaps because I am the talkative wine cask that hides beneath the table

Or perhaps Mount Fu-ch'un who dreams of you from within the clouds

Or perhaps Kung himself who paints you into his painting

January 1974

焚書記

桌前有本書，一本薄薄的書
一本没題没名没有作者的書
在灰色的灰塵下，在金色的金陽中
一本安靜異常的書

在桌前，在我的桌前
一本不知有没誤排缺頁
有没懸疑高潮的書
我，没翻過——

一本不知有無出版年代
有無愛恨生死的書，安安靜靜
在我桌前，没人知道，没人翻過
安靜得可怕，而没人查覺

那薄薄一本好像只有一頁的書
好像一翻，世界就會頓然成灰的書
酷似一扇薄得要命的門
暗含整個地獄，整個天堂

而我没去翻，我没敢去翻
而我不願去開，也不知怎樣去開
在銀色的銀月下，在白色的白雪中
一扇只有我才能看見的書

Book Burning

In front of my desk, a book, a paper-thin book
With no topic, no title, no author
Under the ashen ashes, in the gold of the sun's golden rays
An extraordinarily thin book

In front of the desk, in front of my desk
A book that perhaps has missing or misnumbered pages
That perhaps has suspense and a climax
But I haven't even skimmed it

A book that perhaps has a publication date
That perhaps is filled with love, hate, life, and death, so quiet
Before my desk, no one knows about it, no one has skimmed it
So frightfully quiet, and no one else has realized it

The paper-thin book that seems to have only one page
A book in which the turn of a page might turn the world to ashes
Exactly like a dreadfully thin door
Secretly holding all of hell, all of heaven

But I haven't skimmed it, I haven't dared
And I don't want to open it, I don't even know how to open it
Under the silver light of the silver moon, in the white of the white snow
A book that only I can see

我把它藏入爐火裏
藏入那熊熊的爐火裏
連同我的指甲，我的眼睛
以及一排整齊的，牙齒

六十年八月

I throw it into the stove's flames

Throw it into the stove's blazing flames

Along with my fingernails, my eyes,

And my nice, even teeth

August 1971

大 字 報

——致魏京生及其同伴

他們不斷下令：
要把白雲黏死在廣濶的青天上
要把江河凍結在龜裂的大地上

我們卻暗暗
把大字報張貼進每一雙
空洞無告的眼睛裏
把力量凝聚在每一隻
血脈噴張的拳頭內

只要是白雲，就必須流動飛翔
飛翔成一張張純潔無比的大字報
在大地乾渴決眥的仰望中

每一個字
都將變成溫潤的甘霖一滴
化解千萬條冰封的江河
洶湧的奔聚於我們地道般相連的血脈之內
安靜的沖破至他們以命令糊成的紙堤之外

六八·一

Protest Posters

For Wei Ching-sheng and his companions

They issue the rules continuously:

Nail the white clouds onto the wide blue sky

Paint the frozen rivers onto the parched earth

But stealthily we

Stick the posters onto

The vacant, hopeless eyes

Solidifying our strength in each

Hand with its pulsating veins

If they are white clouds, then let them flow and flap

Flapping as posters of incomparable purity flap

Caught in the hungry, eye-straining gaze of the world

Each word of protest

Becoming a drop of sweet summer rain

Melting a million frozen rivers and streams

Overflowing into hands interlaced with veins like subway maps

Seeping through the paper dikes that their rules have glued together

January 1979

獨門擒龍手

大內擒龍手，武林秘笈
招術簡至不能再簡
然變化複雜神奇奧妙
修練困難艱苦耗時

先置烈火於手掌之內
化顫抖的手掌成搖擺的火焰
再握雙拳於寒冰之中
化鬆動的拳頭成堅凍的隕石

水火交溶之後
手柔，柔如春草初發
手韌，韌如青藤十纏
手勁，勁如老根入土

入土則緩緩聚土成山
聚山成島，以抗大海
入海則細細析浪成波
析波成沙，以馴巉岩

入山入海，可擒毒龍
可擒那狡猾陰殘狠辣險惡的毒龍
毒龍——獨籠，籠破籠開
龍穴遍地，毒龍四出，龍毒四衍

The Hand of the Lone Dragon Slayer

The hand of the imperial dragon slayer, a secret of knighthood

A martial art so simple that it is beyond simplification

Transformed into complexity, mystery and magic

With training so arduous, bitter, and time consuming

First you place the burning fire in your open palm

The quivering palm becomes the flickering flame

And then your fists are thrust into the freezing ice

And the soft palm turns into a solid meteorite

After fire and water have been blended together

The hand is soft, soft as spring grasses

The hand is tough, tough as tangled vines

The hand is firm, firm as roots sunk deep into the earth

Sinking into the soil, slowly gathering it into mountains

Gathering them into an island, thereby opposing the sea

Sinking into the sea, reducing each wave to a ripple

Reducing the ripples to sand, thereby taming the cliffs

Sinking into the sea and mountains, it slays the deadly dragon

Slays that sly, secretly cruel, heartless, dangerous, deadly dragon

Deadly dragon—denned alone, den is broken, den is opened

Everywhere dragon dens, on four sides deadly dragons emerge and spread

龍毒出你的體外，入我的體內
毒龍臥你的墓穴，佔我的墓穴
然！專擒毒龍的大內擒龍手啊
　是武林瑰寶，是江湖奇珍
　思之論之者，一日衆似一日
　尋之覓之者，卻漸寡漸鮮漸無

　時時驚聞復出，復出
　　　將復出
　事實，久已失傳失傳
　　　盡失傳

Dragon venom flows from your body, sinks into mine

The deadly dragon sleeps in your tomb, occupies mine

So it is, the deadly-dragon-slaying hand of the imperial dragon slayer

A treasure of knighthood, a rare jewel of warriors

Those who think and talk about it grow more numerous by the day

Yet those who actually seek it are fewer, rarer, almost unknown

Often one hears of its return, its return

Its imminent return

But indeed, it was lost, lost long ago

Completely lost

喂！你在幹什麼呀

寫詩，就是把自己的
頭腦身體四肢
變成一個活生生
會走路會思想會表演
會到身體外面去冒險的字

就是把自己的夢想
變成一個字兩個字三個字
變成一隊會走會飛
會游泳會潛水的字
與自然界所有的事物交朋友

有時候，寫詩
就是把世界上所有的朋友
組織起來成為一個馬戲團
而你則是那個喜歡表演
高難度特技的
　　　　　　　　空中飛人

Hey, What's Up?

[a poem for children]

In writing poetry you turn your

Mind, body, arms, and legs

Into a living word

One that can walk, think, and put on a show

One that can take more chances than you dare to

You turn your dreams into

A word or phrase

And turn them into a team that can walk and fly

Swim and dive

That can make friends with all living things

In writing poetry you sometimes

Turn all your friends into a circus troupe

And you become the hit of the show

The daring young man on the

                                    flying

Trapeze

Transformations

The recluse turns into wind-blown snow, snow into a waterfall,
falling down again to the pavilion. (Courtesy of Lo Ch'ing)

化魚記

我是衝撞四海激盪九洲

波濤掀天無始無終碧冰洋裏

一條孤傲不群沒名沒姓不言不語

渾身是刺的

怪魚

君若不信，可逕自單騎前去

去問那蘆溝橋外，外患暴漲的外灘

去問那外灘外，半沉半浮的木筏

我曾是那飽經戰亂隨江而下的

木筏

若還不信，便可逆九江溯洞庭穿山峽而上

上至那漢水之濱，柱天鎮地的黃鶴樓

去問那樓頭棲過黃鶴的龍鳳棟樑

我曾是那親身經歷劍吟槍嘯血淚革命的

棟樑

On Piscine Metamorphosis

Standing alone in the crowd nameless and unknown, not
Saying a word, spines covering my body, I am an
In-the-Emerald-Ocean-without-beginning-or-end-full-of-waves-
Brushing-heaven-pounding-the-four-seas-shaking-the-eight-lands
Strange fish

Sir, if you don't believe me, you can simply go as a lone rider

And ask the outer beach outside the Marco Polo Bridge where

    outsiders plundered

Ask that half-sunken wooden raft outside the outer beach

I was that having-my-fill-of-war-went-on-down-the-river

Raft

Sir, if you still don't believe me, then you can make your way up the

    Nine Rivers, through Tung-t'ing Lake, passing up through the Gorges

Up to the beaches of the Han River, to the Yellow Crane Tower that

    stands on earth supporting the heavens

Go ask the pillars and beams carved with dragons and phoenixes on the

    rooftop where the yellow crane alighted

I was myself those having-gone-through-the-bloody-revolution-with-its-

    clanging-swords-and-blasting-guns

Pillars and beams

若硬是不信，則更可跨峨眉泳金沙
翻巴顏喀拉山之絕絕頂，棄長江而問黃河
問黃河源頭那棵九曲八折裂石破雲的龍松
我曾是那識盡人間興衰發聲至哀至悲的
龍松

若至死不信！呵，罷了，罷了，那就罷了
那就讓我狂風暴雨般的，倒下倒下吧
順著那條永無清淨之日的黃河
順著孔丘李白之前便開始奔瀉的洪水奔流到海永不
回頭

永不回頭的我，在不盈不虛
水旱不知的碧冰洋中，從此失了消息
誰也不知道，想不出，找不到，問不著
我究竟是化作了吞舟之巨鯨還是穿針之
細魚

六十一年九月　西雅圖

If you insist on not believing, then you can step across Mount O-mei,
  swim the Kinsha River
Crossing over the loftiest peak of the Banya Kara Range,
  leave the Yangtze behind and go ask the Yellow River
Ask that twisted and turned, rock-splitting, cloud-piercing Dragon Pine
I was that knowing-all-about-the-vicissitudes-of-life-screamed-in-tragic-
  grief
Dragon Pine

But if you would die before you'd believe me, then forget it, just forget it
Let me fall, fall like the pounding rain of a hurricane, let me fall
Swept along by the ever-sullied Yellow River
Swept along by the heavy currents that surged forth before the time of
  Li Po and Confucius flying down to the sea never to
Look back

I, never looking back, in the never-full but never-empty
Emerald Ocean that knows no drought, disappear without a trace
No one knows, can imagine, find, or inquire
Whether I have become a boat-swallowing whale or a needle-threading
Minnow

Seattle, September 1972

兩　棵　樹

在一個鳥雀都不曉得的地方
我看到一棵樹，站在水泥裏
將軍一般——
身段修長而挺直
腰間掛著幾條油漆帶子
胸前佩著許多指路牌子
嚴肅緊張而不知所措的
檢閱一輛快速濺泥而過的車子

在一個陽光都不清楚的地方
一棵樹看到我
俘虜似的……
於重重建築的冷冷監視之下
沒有花果，沒有葉
沒有枝幹，沒有根
沒有，沒有，甚至
沒有名字

59・9

Two Trees

In a place where sparrows never go

I see a tree standing in concrete

Commandantlike erect

Tall and finely built

At its waist a few painted stripes

On its chest road signs dangle

Serious and uptight, with nothing to do

It reviews cars that splash speeding by

In a place sunlight never sees

A tree sees me

Like a prisoner of war . . .

Under the chilling watch of tall buildings all in rows

There are no flowers or fruit, no leaves

No branches, no roots

Nothing, not a thing, not even

A name

September 1970

水牛本紀

我是一團不成形的黑土塊
被一位不知名是泥水匠
遺留在一方綠色繡花的
大毛毯上
被一個無感覺的自我
遺忘在一片雲霧深鎖的
睡眠當中
忽然一陣春雨，漫天而降
寸寸沖刷身上的黑泥
點點溶化僵冷的心胸
在春雷敲打閃電雕刻之下
霍然驚醒的我
以頭角崢嶸之姿
迅速拔地而立

立刻，我用指東劃西的雙角
把自己頭頂的日月
或左或右的雙雙挑起
挑起兩盞圓圓搖晃的燈籠
並感恩的向天地萬物
鄭重宣佈
世上第一隻水牛的誕生

六八・六

附記：司馬遷《史記》爲帝王作「本紀」。水牛爲農民之公僕，造
　　　福百姓，仁德配天，有古聖王之風，當該以「本紀」記其生
　　　平。

The Imperial Annals of the Water Buffalo

I was a black, lumpy clod
Left behind by an unknown bricklayer
On a square, green embroidered
Rug
Forgotten by a numb ego
In a deep, mist-shrouded
Doze
The spring rains poured out of heaven
Soaking into my muddy body inch by inch
Little by little melting my lifeless heart
When thunder's hammer and lightning's chisel
Suddenly brought me to life
I lifted my lofty horns majestically
And rose from the ground to stand

With my eastward- and westward-reaching horns
I took the sun and moon that lay at my head
And carried them left and right on this shoulder pole
Shouldering these two swaying global lanterns
As the myriad creatures toward heaven and earth
Gratefully celebrated
The birth of the first water buffalo

June 1979

Author's note: In Records of the Grand Historian, *Ssu-ma Ch'ien [ca. 145–90 B.C.] invented the imperial annals to record the deeds of the kings and emperors. Since the water buffalo is a servant to the farmer, the bearer of good fortune for the common man, and since he has benevolence equal to heaven and a bearing like that of the ancient sages, he obviously should have his own imperial annals.*

掃 葉 記
　　——贈掃葉珊房主人

和一個會寫詩的人在園裏掃落葉
滿園落葉中的我，也會寫詩
兩個會寫詩的人碰上一個不會寫詩的秋天
便不相干的，以掃把對落葉，相互聊了起來
且無紙無心的，辯來論去吵來掃去
掃成了一張簡筆淡墨的「薄暮掃葉圖」

圖裏，又輕又脆的落葉
輕脆易響，響如少年的夢幻
圖外，又多又亂的落葉
無邊亂飄，飄如逝去的日子
而無論圖裏圖外，我們將在冬雪來前
把拾起的落葉連圖一起，用爐火，細細溫習

熊熊的爐火
可以唬退來襲的寒冷
可以驚走潛入的黑暗
甚至還可以嚇阻那雪前廣大無邊的
寂靜——當我們在寂靜邊緣
把酒論詩的時候……

Raking Leaves

For Yang Mu, my rakish host

In the yard, raking leaves with someone who can write poetry

In this yard full of leaves, I can write poetry too

The two who can write poetry encounter an autumn who can't

But no matter, we face the leaves with our rakes and chat

Without paper or purpose, we debate and discuss, argue and rake

Raking our way into "Raking Leaves in the Dusk," a sketch done in

   gray washes

In the painting, the dry, crackling autumn leaves

Sound like a fantasy of the young

Outside the painting, leaves scattered in disarray

Scattered about with abandon like gone-by days

Inside or out of the painting, we will gather the leaves before the snow

   falls

And burn them along with the painting, warming up for things to come

The blazing fire in the stove

Frightens back the advancing cold

Drives away the deepening darkness

Even halts the endless silence that comes before the snow

And as we stand there at the edge of that silence

Bottles in hand, discussing poetry . . .

把酒的手臂，被火光認眞的映在牆上
猶如把著一柄没有劍刃的長劍
論詩的身影，被火光誤認爲
兩尊高大的羅漢，巍峨而幽黑
殘缺不全的危危立在
南渡後遭兵火洗劫的荒寺裏

而寺外，終於開始下雪了
白色的雪在黑色的空中，沙沙而下
嚇走了殘秋，嚇走了殘夜
一直下到爐不堪火，酒不堪飲，詩不堪論
而所有將落未落的葉子，都被埋盡
爲止

六十二年二月

In the firelight our arms and bottles are cast in silhouettes along the wall

As if we held in our hands the hilts of bladeless swords

These shadows discussing poetry are mistaken by the firelight for

Two tall arhats, gigantic and sullen

Fragmented and wavering they stand in a

Deserted temple gutted by the fires of war after the Tartar invasions

And outside the temple it is finally beginning to snow

White snow in the black night, softly it falls

Frightening away the remnants of autumn, the remnants of night

Falls until the fire can no longer burn, nor the beer be drunk, nor
    poetry discussed

Until all the unfallen leaves that will fall are buried

And then it stops

February 1973

聽　泉　圖

誰都以爲我是一塊
橢圓的卵石
危危立在曲折喧嘩的岸邊
旣無法羽化，也無法鳴叫

其實我原是
大鵬一隻：
雙翼撫雲十萬里
鳴聲穿天九百重

然風雨雷電卻没有
僅僅因爲一隻大鵬而停止
喉頭暗啞，翅羽落盡的
我

不得不抱元守一
還原成初生的石卵一顆
不再光潤閃耀
不再脆薄易碎

歲歲年年日日月月
我只有靜靜坐在岸邊
靜聽那歷經三代兩漢…
…隋唐宋元明清的流水

The Painting "Listening to the Brook"

Everybody thinks I am just

An oval pebble

Perched precariously on the clamorous winding bank

With no way to grow wings, no way to sing

But I am actually

The Great Roc:

My wings brush the clouds for a million miles

My song pierces the nine hundred layers of heaven

And yet, wind and rain, thunder and lightning

Simply because there is only this one Great Roc, never stopped

Me with

Muted voice and fallen feathers

One cannot not hew to primacy

To return to origins, become the river rock first-born

Never again to glitter and shine

Never again to crumble and crack

The years, months, and days go by

And I sit still on the bank

Quietly listening to the annotations of the current

That flows through the Three Epochs, the two Han dynasties . . .

夾雜著各種流派的注疏
渾濁不清的講述
一條魚名爲鯤的故事

六七‧二

註：《莊子》「逍遙遊」：「北冥有魚，其名爲鯤，鯤之大，不
　　知幾千里也。化而爲鳥，其名爲鵬。」

The Sui, T'ang, Sung, Yüan, Ming, and Ch'ing

Murmuring a confused story

Of a fish called K'un

February 1978

Author's note: In the "Distant Travels" chapter of Chuang tzu *it says: "In the Northern Reaches there was a fish; its name was K'un. K'un was so large as to be unknowable. It changed into a bird; its name was the Great Roc."*

入秋十八拍

毛衣脫了又穿
決定穿了，又再一口氣
脫掉

葉子要綠不紅
決心紅了的，便難以一下子
轉綠過來

聽說大寒流
重新開始在北方蠢蠢欲動
徘徊踟躕，將下未下

好在我園子裏種的
都是松、竹、梅、石之屬
箱子裏有的，莫非背包征衣之類

管他大寒流來他不來
我照舊清早起來
穿上新製的中國功夫裝

逕自趕到建國北路
高架公路工程處
準時上我的班

六九‧一一　北望神州有感

Into Autumn: Eighteen Lines

Off with the sweater, then back on

Yes, I'll wear it, then in a bit

Off it goes again

The leaves tend more toward green than red

But deciding on red, it is difficult to turn green again

Just like that

I hear there is a cold front up north

Once again starting to move around a lot

To and fro, back and forth, about to descend, but still not

It is good that in my yard there are

Such things as pine, bamboo, plums, and stones

And in my trunk nothing but backpacks, army clothes, and the like

Whether that old cold front comes or not

I'll still get up early in the morning

Put on my new kung-fu jacket

And go straight off to the construction site

For the overpass on Chien-kuo North Road

Right on time to begin work

November 1980
—longing for Cathay of the far north

變形記

一隻飛撲叫跳的烏鴉
在籠裏，望著我
奇異的眼睛發奇異的光
好像一個突然變成烏鴉的
人——驚恐焦急的張著嘴
似乎是要證明
他是一隻能說話能思想
能看穿我內心的烏鴉

於是，小小斗室裏的我
望著窗外天空
奮奮欲飛的，也跳躍了起來
好像一隻突然變成人的
烏鴉——歡欣鼓舞的張著臂
似乎要證明
自己是一個會飛會翔
會自由進出天地萬物的人

六十一年一月

Metamorphosis

In his cage

A crow beats his wings, jumps and caws

Looking at me with his weird weird eyes

As if he were a man just transformed into a

Crow—mouth wide open with fright and worry

Like he is about to prove

That he is a crow who can think and talk

And look directly into my mind

Meanwhile, from my small shoebox of a room

I look out at the sky

Leaping up and down, I flap my arms

As if I were a crow just transformed into a

Man—joyously spreading his arms in excitement

Like I am about to prove

That I am a man who knows how to fly, how to soar

How to penetrate the myriad transformations of heaven and earth

January 1972

七星山夜宿記

七星山上有青松七棵
七棵青松中唯一走動的
就是我

我邊走邊自手中放出飛鳥七隻
七隻飛鳥閃爍成一行飛白的絕句
醒目的，題在清雅的藍天白雲之間

題在雲天之間的潦草詩句呵
入夜後必將化成七顆……燦爛的星
暗暗顯示出一把隱形的長劍

而其中那唯一接近劍柄
又藏身松內的星星
仍是我

我本該是七隻飛鳥裏的
最後一隻，徘徊在七星山上的松枝間
有如一個誤寫成「妻」的「棲」字，不忍離去

六十年二月

A Night on Mount Pleiades

Green pines on Mount Pleiades, seven of them
And someone moves through the seven green pines
And he is me

As I walk along I set free from my hand birds in flight, seven of them
Seven birds that burst into a flying white line of an ancient quatrain
Eye-catching, inscribed between the elegant blue sky and white clouds

That throwaway verse inscribed between the clouds and sky
Will become seven stars emerging out of the night . . . glittering stars
Dimly revealing an invisible sword

Among them, one star near the hasp
Hides in the pines
And still he is me

I must have been the last of the seven birds in flight
Hesitating among the pine branches on Mount Pleiades
As if mistaking the word "hover" for "lover," I couldn't bear to leave

February 1971

隱 形 記

我站在這裏看你，你不看我
我站在那裏看你，你不看我
我耐心站在所有的角度所有的空間
看你——你都不看我

只有你才能看得到我，而你不看
你不看我，是因爲所有的人都看不到我
所有的人都看不到我，是因爲
你不看我

你不看我，我就不存在
我不存在，哼！那你也就別想存在
你我都不存在了，嘿嘿，那所有的人也……
無法存在

可是，可是即使一切的一切
都瀕臨不存在的危險
你還是不在不乎的不看我
不看看我

於是，我只好乖乖的站在這裏站在那裏
站在一切的內裏，看你看你
我只好把你看成一切，把一切都看成你
我只好把你和一切都看成，我自己

六十年六月

The Invisible Man

I stand here and look at you; you don't look at me
I stand there and look at you; you still don't look at me
I patiently stand in all the corners, in all the spaces
Looking at you—you never look at me

Only you can see me, but you don't even look
You don't look at me because no one can see me
No one can see me because
You don't look at me

You don't look at me, therefore I don't exist
I don't exist, then you don't exist either, so there
Neither you nor I exist, well, well, then no one . . .
There is no way to exist

Yet, yet supposing everything in everything
All approaches the danger of not existing
Would you still not give a damn about looking at me
About taking a look at me

If so, then I might as well stand here quietly, or stand there
Stand in all the interiors, looking at you, looking at you
I might as well look at you and see you as everything, see everything
        as you
I might as well look at you and at everything, seeing it all, as me

June 1971

怨　嘆

老樹彎腰
想要下去玩水
木筏卻想
上岸還原爲樹

而夾在當中的沙岸
卻默默無語
在潮水漲落山巒起伏之間
默默把這些千古以來
不斷的抱怨與嘆息
琢磨成一顆顆渾圓無缺的小沙粒
好像那一個個堅硬無比的舍粒子

然後，默默的證明
而今而後，一切都要消逝
唯此怨嘆無數
必得永生

七一・八

Sighs of Complaint

The old tree hangs over

The water wanting to splash

But the wooden raft wants

To climb back up the bank and be a tree again

Caught between the two of them, the sandy beach

Is silent without a word

Between the ebbing and flooding tide

The rising and falling ridge line

It silently polishes their old unending sighs

Into perfectly smooth flawless grains of sand

Hard like the beads of bodhisattva bones

And it silently proves that

From now on all will disappear

And there will be only those countless sighs

On into eternity

August 1982

松林的月亮

月亮在黑松林後
露出一半
像閉著的眼睛
有著雲形松針的睫毛
所有的東西都不許動呵，不許動
因為，誰一動——
就會把筆直的月光碰彎
把光中透明的神話碰碎
好比碰碎一條精雕薄亮的
玻璃長尺

慢慢升起的月亮，是慢慢睜開的眼睛
一隻悲憫又冷漠的眼睛——没有瞳仁

冷漠的眼睛，雪白閃亮
閃亮點在，黑松林上
使扎人的松林
不得不現出本像
還原成一座雜亂多刺的城市
悲憫的眼睛，朦朧泫然
泫然的懸在，城中心上
使所有受苦受難的人們
做松雲般的夢，結松子般的希望
並且靜靜孕育一座
眞實的松林
衝霜冒雪而綠

六一・八

The Moon in the Pines

From behind the pines the moon
Shows half itself
Like an eye closed
Eyelashes of cloudy needles
Nothing at all should move, no
Because, if anyone moves—
Then the straight rays of the moon will bend
The transparent myths of moonlight will shatter
Shatter just as a thin, finely carved
Crystal rule would shatter

The slowly rising moon is slowly opening its eye
A loving and coldhearted eye—without pupil

The coldhearted eye, snow white and shining
Shines above the pines
The stabbing pines
That cannot help but reveal their original form
Reverting to their confused city of thorns
The loving eye, blurry with tears
Hangs blurry above the city center
Bringing to the distressed and embittered
Dreams like pine clouds, hopes like pine cones
And real pines
To carry silently in their wombs
Green against the frost and snow

August 1972

品　畫　記

一個老人，坐在海邊
和一隻海鳥談心，靜靜的
談平了所有彈不平的波浪
海鳥飛起——心與天平

而年輕的我，整個下午
都守在窗旁，凝坐如一未完成的畫像
在光線變幻不定的背景裏
動也不動的，分析這件事情

當遠遠守護在我身邊的一顆星
爲了怕我怕黑，而俯身下來
照顧我的時候
我才慢慢的察覺：

我依的窗子，原來是牆上掛的
畫框，框中鑲的，原來是一面畫的
鏡子，鏡中反映的，原來是
老去的我，和一隻織在藍地毯上的白鳥

六十年二月

Art Appreciation

An old man sits by the shore

Speaking his mind with a tern, quietly

Speaking the holey waves into a whole

The tern flies off—mind and heaven turning whole

And in my youth I wait all the afternoon

By the window, sit unmoving like an unfinished portrait

Backgrounded by forever changing light

Without the slightest motion, I analyze this thing before me

When a star beside me looks after me from afar

Reaches down to shine on me

Because she's afraid that I'm afraid of the dark

Then I slowly realize:

The window upon which I lean is actually a picture frame

Hung on the wall, and framed therein is actually a painted

Mirror, and reflected in the mirror is actually

Myself getting old, along with a white bird woven on a blue rug

February 1971

Near Postmodern

With a little bow, the lotus leaf says, ''Come on in and see what we have new in the way of blossoms.'' (Courtesy of Lauren A. Allen)

吃西瓜的六種方法

第五種　西瓜的血統

没人會誤認西瓜爲隕石
西瓜星星，是完全不相干的
然我們卻不能否認地球是，星的一種
故而也就難以否認，西瓜具有
星星的血統

因爲，西瓜和地球不止是有
父母子女的關係，而且還有
兄弟姊妹的感情——那感情
就好像月亮跟太陽太陽跟我們我們跟月亮的
一，樣

第四種　西瓜的籍貫

我們住在地球外面，顯然
顯然，他們住在西瓜裏面
我們東奔西走，死皮賴臉的
想住在外面，把光明消化成黑暗
包裹我們，包裹冰冷而渴求溫暖的我們

他們禪坐不動，專心一意的
在裏面，把黑暗塑成具體而冷靜的熱情
不斷求自我充實，自我發展

Six Ways to Eat a Watermelon

The Fifth Way: Watermelon Lineages

No one would confuse a watermelon and a meteorite

Watermelons have nothing in common with the starry night

But we cannot deny that the earth is a satellite of sorts

Therefore it is difficult to say that watermelons and stars have

No family ties

Since watermelons and the earth are not only parent and child

But also love each other like brother and sister

That love is as are the sun and moon, the sun and we,

    we and the moon

A

Like

The Fourth Way: Watermelon Origins

We live on the surface of the earth obviously

And obviously they live in their melon interior

We run to and fro, with our thick skin

Trying to stay on the surface, digesting rays of light

Into the darkness that envelops us, envelops our cold-craving warmth

In *zazen* they concentrate on one thought

Inside sculpting it into calm concrete passion

Always seeking their own fulfillment, their personal development

而我們終就免不了，要被趕入地球裏面
而他們遲早也會，衝刺到西瓜外面

第三種　西瓜的哲學

西瓜的哲學史
比地球短，比我們長
非禮勿視勿聽勿言，勿爲——
而治的西瓜與西瓜
老死不相往來

不羨慕卵石，不輕視雞蛋
非胎生非卵生的西瓜
亦能明白死裏求生的道理
所以，西瓜不怕侵略，更不懼
死亡

第二種　西瓜的版圖

如果我們敲破了一個西瓜
那純是爲了，嫉妒
敲破西瓜就等於敲碎一個圓圓的夜
就等於敲落了所有的，星，星
敲爛了一個完整的，宇宙

而其結果，卻總使我們更加
嫉妒，因爲這樣一來
隕石和瓜子的關係，瓜子和宇宙的交情

But in the end we cannot avoid being pushed into the watermelon

And they sooner or later will burst out of it

The Third Way: Watermelon Philosophy

The history of watermelon philosophy

Is shorter than that of earth, and longer than ours

Not practicing see no evil, hear no evil, say no evil, no thing

Having nothing to do with each other

The watermelon haves and have nots

No envy for ovum, no disdain for egg

Neither oviparous, nor viviparous

Comprehending the principle of finding life in death

the watermelon does not fear invasion, or cringe

Before destruction

The Second Way: Watermelon Domains

If we were to smash a watermelon

It would be for jealousy

Smashing a watermelon is the same as bashing a global night

And that is to dash all the stars from the star-filled sky

And to mash the entire universe flat

And as a result we would be more jealous

Yet, since then

The relationship of meteorite and melon seed, the friendship of melon
    seed and universe

又將會更清楚，更尖銳的
重新撞入我們的，版圖

第一種　吃了再說

59.12

Would be even clearer, and would again sink its

Blade deep into our domain

The First Way: Let's Eat, Then Talk

December 1970

梯　子

梯子
在冷牆角
在菓樹下
空空的斜著
斜斜的靠著

所有的梯子
都是這樣的
無論是在被利用之前
或利用之後

七一・八

The Ladder

The ladder

Is in the cold corner of the wall

Underneath the fruit tree

Blankly slanting

Slantedly leaning

All ladders

Are like this

Both before they are used

And after

August 1982

驚醒一條潛龍

——序曲

各位前輩，諸位高手
請稍安勿躁，請且慢動手，且慢慢聽我道來
在下兄弟敝人我，雖非壞蛋，然脾氣卻壞得很
實乃一名正派不容，邪道不許的狂徒

看誰都不順眼，尤其看自己不順
天天忙著把自家塑起砸爛再塑起的
我——今年較王勃大比荊軻小
與李廣把臂，和岳飛同調

常常隻身闖關東，但又喜歡把江南的草原踩得呱呱亂響
霹，靂，拍，啦，在身後開出各色各樣的花花朵朵出來
年年單騎走天涯，卻又總愛以兇殘慈悲的眼神
日，日，月，月，輪流照遍萬事萬物

是故，薔薇上有我粗暴的腳印
荊棘中有我溫柔的吻痕
颱風中有我駭人無比的寂靜
深海底有我狂亂懾魂的嘯聲

Waking the Sleeping Dragon

—Prelude

My elders of superior training

Calm yourselves, cease your havoc, still your hand, listen to me

Your squire, your page, I'm not a bad sort, but my temper is bad enough

A crazed disciple accepted by neither the virtuous nor the villainous

I can't bear the countenance of anyone, especially myself

Every day I spend sculpting, then destroying and sculpting again

Myself—bigger than the writer Wang Po, smaller than the assassin

Ching K'o

Arm in arm with General Li Kuang, singing the same song as Yüeh Fei

the hero

Forever seeking adventures in the Northwest, then gleefully tromping

through the flowers in the South, crushing them, making them scream

Behind me in various hues and kinds, the flowers blossom

bunch by bunch

Every year I go as a lone horseman to the edges of the sky, always

finding delight in casting about my evil eye

Day by day, month by month, rolling on, observing all things, all affairs

Thus, my rapacious footprints are found among the roses

On the thorns the soft traces of my kisses

In the typhoon is my most frightening silence

And my crazed, soul-piercing scream at the bottom of the sea

我縱橫左右，上下古今
告訴你！世間最最過癮的事
莫過於在天南地北，歷朝歷代的臉上
蓋我那既朱且紅發光發熱的，章子

我緩伸左手，劍閃如電，左手成劍
我舒揚右手，蓮展如詩，右手成蓮
軀幹修長——我是一道身手矯健的飛瀑
心境幽邃，我是一井紋風不動的泉水
於井未湧瀑未飛花未生電未閃之際
我原是一顆渾圓欲滴的露珠……渾圓一如地球

地球是第一個不透明，我是第一個透明
透透明明，我在不透明的地上，把該說的都儘情說盡
諸位！要是有不服氣的，就亮傢伙吧
廢話少說——看招

Back and forth I cross the kingdoms, up and down I pass through time

The thing in this world that most satisfies my passion

Is stamping my vermilion, heat and light radiating signature

On the world's expanse, on the face of the ages

My sword flashes like lightning, my left hand extends into a blade

The lotus unfolds like a poem, my right hand raised, becomes a lotus

I stand tall and lean, a cascade of flying arms and hands

My heart is deep and distant, I am a wellspring that the winds can't ripple

Before this spring surged, cascades flew, flowers grew,

and lightning flashed

I was a pearl of dew about to drop . . . round like the earth

The earth is the opaque, I am the transparent

I am transparently in the opaque world, saying all that should be said

with emotion

My dear sirs, if any of you disagree, then watch my shining friend here

Hold your tongue. On guard!

茶杯定理

定 理 一

設圓圓茶几上

有　杯茶

設一杯是熱

一杯是冷

則圓圓房間裏必會

有　個人

一個還少

另一則老

上述定理

圓圓地球上的任何壹人

只要泡壹杯茶

安安靜靜，定可證明

定 理 二

設茶杯非水井

則透明的杯子

與不透明的井

不但等高，而且同底

The Teacup Theorems

Theorem 1

Supposing that on a round table for tea

There are   teacups

Supposing one cup is hot

And one is cold

Then, certainly in the round room

There are   people

And one is still young

Another has grown old

As for the theorem above

Any one person on this round earth

Only has to brew one cup of tea

In quietude and it is proved

Theorem 2

Supposing a teacup is not a well

Then a transparent teacup

Compared to an opaque well

Is not only of a different height, but also of a different base

無論底是地心還是手掌心
無論高是七尺長還是十八層深
杯子總被人握著，緊緊的
一如地球總握著水井

杯子因握著的人不同
而有千千萬萬，不同的性格
握著水井的地球卻因水井的不同
而永遠只有一個，一種性格

井邊壹個手握杯子的人
想到這裏，把水喝完
讓手中的杯子回井中去
讓自家的身子回家中去

定　理　三

設手中有個杯子
則必須用心拿著
若不小心，打破杯子
那就打破了——

No matter if the base is the center of the earth or of one's hand

No matter if it is seven feet tall or eighteen layers deep

A cup is always held firmly in hand

Just as the earth holds onto a well

Because the people who hold cups are different

So there are a million different kinds

Because wells are different, the earth that holds them

Is forever singular and of one type

When someone beside the well who holds a cup

Realizes this, he finishes his tea

Lets the cup return to the well

Lets his self return home

Theorem 3

Supposing there is a cup in one's hand

Then one must hold it intently

For if one is not careful, he will break it

That means he will break:

一杯牛奶，一杯溫暖的愛
一杯可樂，一杯衝動的氣泡
一杯檸檬，一杯酸澀的感情思想
一杯烈酒，一杯無法追憶的往事年代

手中破了的杯子，鋒利割手
心中碎了的苦樂，尖銳割心
是悲杯，還是杯悲
是杯悲杯？還是悲悲悲？

悲得是，所有的愛所有的氣泡
所有的感情思想，往事年代
皆將化爲細小堅硬且透明的哀怨
化爲沉澱在杯底的濕黏灰塵

打碎一杯灰塵
也就等於＝打破了自己
因爲，杯子易碎
一如打破杯子的，人

A cup of milk, a cup of warm love

A glass of Coke, a glass of volatile fizz

A tumbler of lemonade, a tumbler of sour thoughts

A shot of liquor, a shot of nostalgia

The pieces of the cup that breaks in one's hand cut

The shards of the joy that shatters in one's heart cut too

But is it the cut of the cup, or the cup's cut

Is it the cup's cut for the cup, or the cut's cut for the cut?

No, the cut is for all the love and all the fizz

All the sour thoughts and nostalgia

That will transform into hard, transparent resentment

Into a sticky grime that precipitates into the bottom of the cup

To break a grimy cup

Is to break oneself

Because the cup shatters as easily as he who breaks

It

December 1970

日　出

我看到一輪太陽

從萬山之中

從叢林之中

從瓦屋之中

從房間之中

哦不！從我的

頭顱之中

冒了

出來

居然是

方形的

上面刻著

兩個易懂的篆字：

Sunrise

I saw the sun's great orb

Rise

Out of the myriad mountains

Out of the thick forests

Out of the tiled roofs

Out of the room

But, no. Out of my head

It rose

And

Indeed

It was

My chop

Carved with

Two simple and square characters

多次觀滄海之後再觀滄海

平平坦坦的大海上
好像什麼都沒有

好像什麼都沒有的大海上
居然真的什麼都沒有

就是因為原來什麼都沒有
才知道根本什麼都沒有

可是平平坦坦的大海之上
的確什麼都沒有嗎？

什麼都沒有的海上啊
當然是什麼都沒有

平平坦坦的大海之上
果然渾然自自然然的是什麼都沒有

註：曹孟德建安十二年作
〈步出夏門行〉，首章
〈觀滄海〉，其辭如下：
　　東臨碣石
　　以觀滄海
　　水何澹澹

Once More Looking out at the Deep Blue Sea after Looking out at the Deep Blue Sea Many Times Before

On the calm and expansive sea

There seems to be nothing at all

On the sea where there seems to be nothing at all

There is in fact simply nothing at all

It is just because there is after all nothing at all

That we know there was originally nothing at all

But on the calm and expansive sea

Is there actually nothing at all?

On the sea where there is nothing at all

Of course there is nothing at all

On the calm and expansive sea

There is expectedly completely naturally nothing at all

Author's note: Ts'ao Ts'ao's first poem in the "Walking out of Summer Gate" series, called "Looking out at the Deep Blue Sea," was written in the seventeenth year of the Chien-an period [A.D. 212]. Its lyrics go like this:

Eastward we approach Stele Mountain
From there looking out at the deep blue sea
How peaceful and broad is its water

山島竦峙
樹木叢生
百草豐茂
秋風蕭瑟
洪波湧起
日月之行
若出其中
星漢燦欄
若出其表
幸甚至哉
歌以詠志

後記：
這是我第一次
用電腦文書處理系統
寫詩
其中「竦峙」兩字
是用造字系統
畫出來的

Alpestrine spires stand on the mountain isle
Trees grow in profusion
The myriad plants are abundant
The autumnal wind sighs
Heavy waves surge
The course of sun and moon
Seems to start from there
The river of stars burning bright
Seems to rise from within it
How very fortunate
Songs enchant intent

Also Note:
This is the first poem I wrote
with a Chinese word processor
Since the characters for "alpsetrine" were not
contained in its memory
when I came to write the above note
I had to create them with the character-graphics program

三斷論法

一、書房書房

書

我坐在書房裏，守書看書
把大大的書房，看小守小
小小的書房，鎖我關我
把自高自大的我，關瘦鎖老
老瘦的我，無能的癱在書架上
成了一冊薄薄的書，做著各式各樣的夢
各式各樣的夢，是各種各類的老鼠
為求存活，不斷啃咬著各型各版的書籍
各型各版的書籍，距我近得遙遠，熟得陌生
近如我散落在四方的兄弟
陌如我飄零在異地的肢體

房

我臥在書房裏
拒絕幻想方方的書房是方形的舟
拒絕幻想我是方形舟中
唯一的舵手，唯一的船長
更拒絕承認所有的典籍老鼠
是我唯一的乘客
我望著窗外漸增漸強的風雨
感覺那微微的地震，遠遠的山洪

Syllygisms

1. Reading Room Reading Room

Reading

I sit in the reading room looking after and reading my books

Looking after and reading the large reading room into smallness

The small reading room shutting and locking me up

The egomaniac me shut and locked into old frailty

The frail old me collapsed and powerless on the bookcase

Becomes one thin volume that dreams all types of dreams

And all those dreams are all kinds of rodents

That keep themselves alive by incessantly chewing up all the editions

And all those editions are so distantly close and familiarly strange to me

Close like brothers who are scattered to the corners of the earth

Strange like my four limbs that are drifting in distant lands

Room

I lie in my reading room

Denying the hallucination that the square room is a square-rigged ark

Denying the hallucination that I am the ark's

Only navigator, only captain

And denying even more that all those bookish rodents

Are my only passengers

Gazing out the window at the growing wind and rain

I feel that slight tremor, the flash flood in the distant mountains

我知道，我早已擱淺，早已破敗
早已沉澱，早已封埋，但——
那決非是在悲壯驚險荒涼的海上

書　房

然無須相瞞的是
我確確實實無法衝出這小小的房間
正如我無法衝出我的腦間
我無法清除房中腐爛的報紙與典籍
正如我無法清除週身的病痛與堆積的骨骼
偶爾鬆動的肋骨與盤骨清脆的碰響
會令我想起光，想起愛
想起那比光比愛更遙遠的——神
而一隻老鼠的尖叫
卻又會令我憶起自己的身世
那以文字組成的身世，那慢慢漫漶成省略號……的身世
於是，我期待著我渴望著
期待渴望一次完全的崩塌，完全的毀滅
那將是我一生中唯一發聲的，嘆息

And know that I am already grounded, already demolished

Already precipitated, already buried, but—

It definitely did not happen on a grief-stricken, frightening, vast sea

Reading Room

Thus what I need not keep from you is that

I actually have no way to break out of this small room

Just as I have no way to break out of my own mind

I have no way to cleanse the room of the rotting paper and tomes

Just as I have no way to cleanse the body's sickness and accumulated

    bones

Occasionally the clacking sound of free-floating ribs and pelvic arches

Brings to mind light, brings to mind love

Brings to mind something even more distant than light and love—

    the gods

But then the squeal of rodents

Also conjures up my own life

That life built of script, that life that slowly crumbles into . . . ellipses

Thereupon, I wait on, thirst for

Wait and thirst for the complete collapse, the total destruction

That will be my life's only sound, a sigh

二、流行歌曲

流

告訴我
風雨中欲放的花是怎樣的花朵
雷雨中欲斷的樹是怎樣的樹木
雲雨中欲昇的月是怎樣的月亮
告訴我
沒有支流的河是怎樣的河流
沒有倒影的湖是怎樣的湖泊
沒有生物的海是怎樣的海洋
告訴我告訴我（而我們都是自私自利）
　　　　　　（追求財色名勢的一群）
　　　　　　（我們都是……………）

行

告訴我
充塞夢中狂放的慾是怎樣的慾望
沖出大腦怒放的思是怎樣的思想
衝入體內爆放的子是怎樣的子彈
告訴我
缺乏愛信的生是怎樣的生殖
缺乏幻滅的生是怎樣的生命
缺乏險難的生是怎樣的生活
告訴我告訴我（而我們都是野生勃勃）
　　　　　　（追求長生不老的一群）
　　　　　　（我們都是……………）

2. Hot Pop Songs

Hot

Tell me

About the flowers that are about to blossom in the windblown rain

About the trees that are about to crack in the lightning and rain

About the moonlight that is about to burst through this clouded rain

Tell me

What kind of river is a river without branches

What kind of lake is a lake without reflection

What kind of sea is a sea without living things

Tell me, tell me (but we are all selfish and self-serving)

        (A mob in search of wealth, sex, fame, and power)

        (We are all . . .)

Pop

Tell me

About those wild and free desires that fill your dreams

About the raging thoughts that pour out of your mind

About the fiery bullets that explode out of your body

Tell me

What kind of creation is a life without love and hope

What kind of lifetime is a life that denies fantasies

What kind of living is life that does not like danger

Tell me, tell me (but we are all mad animals)

        (A herd in search of immortality)

        (We are all . . .)

歌曲

告訴我呀
失去坐位的椅子是怎樣的椅子
失去傢俱的房間是怎樣的房間
失去屋頂的屋子是怎樣的屋子
失去兒女的母親是怎樣的母親
失去妻子的丈夫是怎樣的丈夫
失去人民的國家是怎樣的國家
失去人類的地球是怎樣的地球
失去地球的太陽是怎樣的太陽
失去繁星的宇宙是怎樣的宇宙
告訴我呀告訴我，告訴我——
我們都是默默無聞
追求安逸死亡的一群
我們都是

Songs

Yes, tell me

What is a chair denied its seating

A room denied its furniture

A rooftop denied its roof

A mother denied her children

A husband denied his wife

A country denied its people

A world denied humankind

A sun denied its earth

A universe denied its stars

Yes tell me, tell me—

We are all laboring in obscurity

A gang in search of comfort and death

We are all

一座越長越高的山

爬上山頂時
一堆鳥糞落在頭上

那飛鳥和我一樣
也只不過是經過而已
我想擡頭而没擡頭——

因爲我看到
一個全然陌生的人
從我體内走出

一人一鳥
一天一地的
遠去

使楞在山頂的我
與鳥糞化合爲一

六五・一一

So Grows the Mountain

When I climb the mountain peak
A bird turd drops on my head

That bird is like me
Just passing through, that's all
I want to raise my eyes, but don't

Because I see
A total stranger
Walk out from inside of me

A man, a bird
Are as far apart as
A heaven, an earth

Making me, bird-brained on the mountain peak,
One with bird turd

November 1976

一封關於訣別的訣別書

卿卿如晤：
提起筆
就想給你寫信
抓起一張紙
三行兩行的
一寫就寫到了
這裏
既然寫到了這裏
也只有寫到
這裏了
就此打住
敬祝
平安愉快

意洞手書
民國七十五年
三月二十八日夜
西曆一九八六年
三月二十七日夜
黃曆四六八四年
三月二十六日夜

A Good-bye Epistle about Good-bye

My Dearest,

Taking up my pen

In order to write you this letter

I grab a sheet of paper

And write two or three lines down to

Here

Since I've written down to here

And only

Down to

Here

I'll stop now

Wishing you

Many happy returns

Sincerely I pen this

The evening of March 28

In the seventy-fifth year of the Republic

The evening of March 27

1986 in the Western calendar

The evening of March 26

4684 by the Chinese almanac

附筆：
信中所寫
絕對與信中
所沒有寫的
任何事物
無關

又及：
此信
萬一被
史學家
考古家
批評家
編選家
或偷窺狂
看到了
敬請
視而不見
高抬貴手

PS

What is written in this letter

Definitely has nothing to do

With anything

That is not written

In this letter

PPS

If this letter is

By chance

Seen by

A historian

Archaeologist

Critic

Anthologist

Or crazy thief

I respectfully request

You not pay it any mind

If you would be so kind

Translator's Notes

Yang Mu

King Wu's Encampment: A Suite of Songs

King Wu was one of the founders of the Western Chou dynasty (1122–770 B.C.). This poem refers to the attack he led from the west against the Shang state in 1122 B.C., in which he crossed the Yellow River at Meng-chin. I discuss this poem in the essay following this section.

Line 1. The date is given in traditional lunar month and independent sixty-day cycle designations: the fifty-fifth day of the cycle that fell in the first lunar month.

Line 17. The original quotes *The Book of Songs* regarding the disruption of war; I substitute the Biblical reference to suggest the intertextual weight of the line.

Continuing Han Yü's "Mountain Stones"

In "Mountain Stones," the T'ang poet Han Yü (768–824) describes his visit to a temple in the mountains ("The monk said how fine the wall paintings of the temple were / Illuminating their rare splendor with a torch"). Han Yü's poem is quite melancholy and philosophical.

Poem 1

Line 7. This refers to an imperial coup at the beginning of the T'ang dynasty, in which Li Shih-min killed his brothers in order to assume the throne.

Line 11. Ch'u was an ancient southern state in the middle reaches of the Yangtze River, wherein lies Mount Heng, one of the five sacred mountains of China. The state was known for its rich religious culture associated with shamanism, and as the home of China's first known poet, Ch'ü Yüan (3d cent. B.C.).

Poem 2

Line 4. The poet known for his training in sword fighting is Li Po (701–762).

Line 10. "Fu-chou" probably refers to Tu Fu's "Yüeh-yeh," written for his wife.

Last line. Ssu-ma Hsiang-ju (179–117 B.C.) was a Han dynasty poet famous for his rhapsodies (*fu*).

Bring on the Wine

The title was derived originally from the first-century-B.C. ritual poem quoted in the epigraph (whose concluding lines are obscure), but the title also has been used for many later literati poems.

Poem 4

Line 6. The woman's self-introduction is written in Japanese.

Line 10. Names of major hexagrams of *The Book of Change* (I Ching), specifically hexagrams 1, 2, 23, and 24.

Line 14. *Odoriko* is Japanese for "dancing girl."

Line 19. *Suiyobi* is Japanese for "Wednesday."

Surprise Lilies

The name of the flower is apparently Yang's neologism, "catch-you-off-guard flower," but I could not resist "surprise lily."

Six Songs to the Tune "Partridge Skies"

"Partridge Skies" is a traditional tune (*tz'u*) title. The subtitle of the fourth poem is derived from a poem in *The Book of Songs* that refers to a type of climbing vine as a metaphor for a wife clinging to her husband for support.

An Autumnal Prayer to Tu Fu

Tu Fu was a major poet, some say the greatest, of traditional China.

Line 3. Place names in Szechwan; refers to uprisings in the 760s.

Lines 4–6. Places where Tu Fu lived after leaving Ch'eng-tu in 765.

Line 8. The title of a poem in which Tu Fu writes of seeing a young woman dance, dated the nineteenth of the tenth month of 767.

Line 15. Tu Fu died in Lei-yang.

Line 18. According to legend, Tu Fu died after being rescued from starvation and fed beef and pure wine.

A Love Poem

Lines 13 and 15. These are quotations from the opening lines of the classical poem "In Praise of the Orange Tree," attributed to Ch'ü Yüan.

Kaohsiung

Kaohsiung is a large port city in southern Taiwan.

A Stand of Rice

Line 15. In Chinese the garlic plant is sometimes called a "narcissus that doesn't flower" (because of its similar foliage), and by extension means "to play innocent." The line here actually reads, "We discover that the plant that is not blossoming really is a narcissus." I have used the Greek myth since it seems oddly appropriate.

Zeelandia

Zeelandia is the Dutch name for the southern Taiwanese town of Tainan, where the Dutch began their colonization of the island in the seventeenth century.

Poem 4

Lines 8–9. Isla Formosa (Beautiful Island) is the name the Portuguese gave to the island when they came in the sixteenth century.

From the "Nine Arguments"

"Nine Arguments" is a sequence of poems attributed to Sung Yü (1st cent. B.C.).

Conversation Class

Note that the original poem is extremely structured, with each line of ten characters and each stanza of six lines; this is a device rarely used by Yang and formalizes the somewhat casual language of the poem.

From "Fourteen Sonnets for Ming-ming"

Ming-ming is a diminutive for the name of Yang's son, Ch'ang-ming (Bruce, in English), who also appears in the poem "International Dateline Concerto."

Moon over Pass Mountain

Numerous literati imitations of the traditional song (*yüeh-fu*) "Moon over Pass Mountain" were written during the medieval period, Weng Shou's late-T'ang poem being nearly the last of these. Yang Mu's poem is much in the spirit of these melancholy poems that depict life on the northern borders of China. The lines of the first and last stanzas in the original are all end-rhymed (-*ang*), which is rare in Yang's poetry and contributes to the archaic atmosphere of the poem.

Gazing Down

Li-wu Creek cuts Toroko Gorge, a deep, spectacular slice in the marble mountains on the east coast of Taiwan, not far from Yang's hometown.

Song of Yesterday's Snow

Line 16. "The T'ao-t'ie monster" refers to an animalistic face that is a part of Shang dynasty bronze decoration dating from the second millenium B.C.

Someone Asked Me about Truth and Justice

Line 13. "Mystery Pagoda script" refers to a standard script model established during the T'ang dynasty by Liu Kung-chüan.

Lo Ch'ing

The Rice Song

This poem appears in a grade-school textbook issued by the Ministry of Education in Taiwan, and thus is, especially among children and younger people in Taiwan, one of Lo's best-known poems.

Bizarre Manifestations of the Dharma

This sequence also exists as a series of paintings on album leaves (now belonging to the St. Louis Art Museum), which is reproduced in my article "Lo Ch'ing's Poetics of Integration: New Configurations of the Literati Tradition," *Modern Chinese Literature* 2.2: 143–67.

Last poem. The *bodhi* tree is where the historical Buddha attained enlightenment.

A Silent Prayer

Lo's footnote identifies the text of the television advertisement as "With a telephone, you can reach someone far away." I substitute "Reach out and touch someone," which appears in a U.S. advertising campaign for Bell Systems.

Fluorescent Lights

The poem is built on a slight pun: the Chinese word for "fluorescent light" is "sun(light) light" (*jih-kuang teng*). The concluding quote actually reads, "Please turn on the fluorescent light."

The Avenging Ghost

P'u Sung-ling (1640–1715) was a writer of classical short stories, the best known of which are the ghost stories in his *Strange Stories from a Chinese Studio* (Liao-chai chih-i). Here Lo uses those images and language to write his own ghoulish poem.

Bitter Tea

The title is actually the name of a type of tea, *k'u ch'a; t'u k'u* (the bitterness of the *t'u* plant), in the epigraph, is a metaphor for life's hardship, thus my translation. Shen Chien-shih (1885–1947) was a traditional scholar and museum curator associated with Peking University and the Palace Museum in Peking.

Reading Paintings in the Cloud-Nourishing Studio

Kung Hsien (1618–1689) was a painter of the Nanking school.

Protest Posters

Wei Ching-sheng was a student leader in the 1979 "Democracy Wall" protests in Beijing. As of this writing he is languishing in prison, and is reported to be in very poor physical and mental health.

On Piscine Metamorphosis

The poem generally describes a mad circuit through China, more or less proceeding up the Yangtze and then down the Yellow River to the sea.

Line 2. The Marco Polo Bridge (outside Peking) is where the Japanese invasion of China officially began in 1937.

Line 6. Tung-t'ing Lake is a major lake in the middle of the Yangtze River system. Above it are the famous mountain gorges, commonly called the Three Gorges.

Line 7. The Han is a northern tributary to the Yangtze. The Yellow Crane Tower is an ancient monument located in the area.

Line 11. Mount O-mei is on the upper reaches of the Yangtze and is a famous site for Buddhist pilgrimages. The Kinsha is the source river for the Yangtze.

Line 12. The Banya Kara are the far western mountains from which the Yangtze and Yellow rivers emerge.

Raking Leaves

See the essay following this section for an explanation of my adaption of the Chinese pun involving the title and dedication.

The Painting "Listening to the Brook"

Author's note. *Chuang-tzu* is a Taoist text (ca. 4th cent. B.C.) known for its humorous philosophic anecdotes.

A Night on Mount Pleiades

In Chinese the term "seven stars" actually refers to Ursa Major, not the Pleiades.

Line 15. The graphic/phonetic pun in Chinese is between the words "roost" and "wife" (*ch'i*).

Six Ways to Eat a Watermelon

"The Fourth Way," line 6. *Zazen* is the Buddhist, especially Zen, discipline of sitting in meditation.

Waking the Sleeping Dragon

Lines 7–8. Ching K'o, who attempted to assassinate China's infamous tyrannical first emperor, Ch'in Shih Huang-ti (d. 210 B.C.); Li Kuang (d. 99 B.C.), a tragic-heroic general; and Yüeh Fei (1103–1141), a famous patriotic general, all were known for their martial heroism and tragic ends. Wang Po (649–676) was a writer who died in exile in the deep South.

Syllygisms

Lo puns on the Chinese term "syllogism" (*san tuan*, lit., "three steps"), by using the homophonous character "interruption" for *tuan*. The English pun on "silly" seems of an appropriate level, even though the effect is somewhat different.

Density and Lucidity

The Poetics of Yang Mu and Lo Ch'ing

The poetics of Yang Mu and Lo Ch'ing contrast and comple-
ment each other in the same way that their lives and personalities
do. By exploring their particular creative talents and intellectual
interests, Yang and Lo have developed individual poetic voices
that, each in its own way, embrace the cosmopolitan and native,
and when considered together yield an aesthetic whole.

First we should note that, despite the differences between
these two poets, there are many things that bind them together. As
their biographies indicate, both are broadly read in the literature of
the world and of the Chinese tradition. Because of his professional
circumstances, this is especially so for Yang. When he speaks of
Greek, German, and Italian literature, this is not merely from a
passing acquaintance, but rather from profound exposure to them
(including his own major translation projects). The two poets
share a familiarity with the Chinese classical tradition, but Yang's
is more literary, while Lo's includes strong affinities with the visual
arts. Lo began his study of Chinese ink painting as a young child;
his artwork displays both superb technical skill and pathbreaking
revisions of the medium. In some ways Lo sees himself first as a
painter, then as a poet. This distinction significantly informs the
poetry of the two writers. Yang's poetry is always more "literary,"
focusing on language and intertextual complexity, while Lo's is
more "visual," exploiting conceptual patterns and conceits. This is
attested to by their introductory essays in this volume and is also
the rationale behind the different types of "illustrations" I use here
to preface their poems. In addition, both Yang and Lo are closely
tied to socio-political developments in Taiwan. Yang lives in the
United States, but his Taiwanese heritage aligns him with the po-
litical interests of the native Chinese population of the island. Lo,
on the other hand, comes from a mainland family, but obviously
loves the island and continues to live there, which keeps him in
close contact with its daily life.

But the difference between the poetries of Yang and Lo is fun-
damental, and transcends not only their specific biographies but

also the conditions of their times. Their poetries offer two distinct, equally successful responses to the demands of modernity in Taiwan.

While the beginnings of modern Chinese poetry might be pushed back to the turn of the century, its emotional and substantial origins are in the May Fourth political/literary movement of 1919 and the decade thereafter. What began as a student-led demonstration against the ill-treatment of China in the hands of foreign powers at the end of the First World War (in which China was allied with and then exploited by its victors), this movement soon took on dimensions of widespread social and cultural reform. Part of that reform was the promotion of a literature in the vernacular language. Within fifteen years this led to some of the most powerful vernacular prose fiction China has ever seen, the best-known examples of which are the short stories of the 1920s and 1930s by Lu Hsün, Mao Tun, and Shen Ts'ung-wen. In poetry, things moved much more slowly, and while those years produced a number of fine poets, with Hsü Chih-mo and Wen I-to always at the top of the list, there was a sense of the unattainable in the poetry of the vernacular language. While the prose fiction of the short story moved on to other forms and styles, the success of the earlier work always provided a foundation for those innovations; poetry, on the other hand, moved on with less confidence, always unsure of its success. This difference can be accounted for if we look back to the classical tradition from and against which the vernacular literature arose.

The May Fourth reform focused its discontent on the classical language, which had been the privileged literary vehicle for nearly two millennia. The reformers declared it a moribund language, its potential exhausted by centuries of reworking the same materials: they saw it unfit to meet the challenge of the modern world, which sat on their doorsteps in the guise of Western science, industrialization, and imperialism. While these accusations were widespread, the genres most disparaged were poetry and the formal octopartite essay. This was a result not only of their ossified condition, but also of the privileged position they held in the elite Mandarin culture of traditional China. These two genres were integral to the promotion and maintenance of the ruling class: they were used in the civil service examination system and sustained the socio-political intercourse of that powerful class.

The ability of modern prose fiction to find a voice in the vernacular language also must be viewed in the environment of late imperial culture. The success of the modern short story lies in the simple fact that vernacular or near-vernacular fiction had been written for centuries in China—most importantly in the classical "novel." And since this genre was *not* a privileged one, it was free from the taint of the bankrupt Mandarin culture that had brought China to its knees at the beginning of the twentieth century. Because it was a genre officially disparaged by the ruling elite, and because prose fiction in the West had been associated with industrialization and modernization, it was a perfect vehicle and voice for the revolution that swept China.

In this environment, the circumstances of poetry were particularly complicated. Easily disparaged as a worn-out genre, poetry still held special regard in the Chinese imagination. This was especially so for the intellectual elite who not only knew the power that the genre had once held (conventionally associated with the great T'ang poets Li Po and Tu Fu), but also were familiar with the very different poetic traditions of the West. The problem was and is the vernacular language. Simply put, while this prosaic language might, nearly by definition, well fit the purposes and forms of prose fiction, it was difficult to make it rise to the heights that poetry demanded. Classical language might have been dead, but its earlier splendor was always a haunting presence, and it most haunted the poetic genres. At its best the language of classical poetry is charged with lyrical density and simultaneously is filled with perspicuity. Classical Chinese poetry can be truly sublime. Prejudice toward the classical language and its poetry is still remarkably widespread, although perhaps not always well informed. In Taiwan, for example, not only do most conservative academics feel that modern poetry does not warrant serious attention, but even taxi cab drivers will commonly express their definite preference for classical poetry (and like taxi cab drivers the world over, they are full of opinions)—why should one bother with this modern stuff when there are volumes and volumes of unread "real poetry," they ask. Thus, poets who turned to the vernacular were placed in a double bind. They were expected to write poetry in a language whose associations were totally apoetic, and they were forbidden to write in the language that was for them synonymous with poetry. The quantum leap that this project required was for many debilitating. It was like asking the dumb to speak. This was a "crisis of language" of an immense order.

While the modern Chinese poet's dilemma has often been compared to that of Dante and especially Goethe, who struggled with the demands and gifts of a new literary language, it would seem that the Chinese situation is even more desperate than the Italian or German. First of all, while Chinese vernacular language is radically different from classical Chinese in structure, vocabulary, and syntax, it shares an identical script and that script is constructed on the "morphographic" level. This means that at any point vernacular language can slip back into the classical without disturbing the surface of the text. Of course, this can be a powerful tool in the hands of the gifted poet; he can energize the vernacular language with touches of classical poetic diction and vocabulary. But the danger is also obvious. The power of classical poetic language can overtake the vernacular, creating a poem that may be modern in shape but classical in language and vision. That danger is compounded by the fact that the Chinese poetic tradition is not only extremely long, but is continuous and nearly uniformly strong. To promote radical change in literary style or language at any given time was to force that change onto an omnipresent, nearly omnipotent, literary world. The power of that world to repossess the text was immense. A number of early poets who attempted to use the vernacular language gave up and returned to classical forms. Others turned to prose, while still others wrote poems that claim "substantially I am really a cat, there has just been some mistake as far as my external form is concerned." Among those early poets, the most successful were often those who had extensive exposure to both Chinese and Western poetry (as opposed to prose fiction). This dual exposure gave them a model of poetry in the vernacular, and also allowed them to control the power of the classical language, both to use it to their own ends and to prevent it from repossessing their work.

There were a number of strong vernacular poets in the 1920s and 1930s, with Hsü Chih-mo leading the list of those whose exposure to Western (English) poetry was significant, and Wen I-to as the one with consummate control of the Chinese classical tradition. They, and others like them, explored new thematic realms in poetry, especially romanticism, eroticism, and social alienation. That both were killed while still young men (Hsü in a plane crash and Wen by an assassin) is emblematic of the tumultuous times in which they lived. In the late 1930s and 1940s the war against Japan, World War II, and then the Chinese civil war diverted substantial poetic activity to the various political causes and to prose writing. It was not until the coming of Communist rule to the mainland and the retreat of the KMT to Taiwan that there was again an environment (or two environments, as it were) in which poetry could flourish.

On the mainland, poetry took up the socialist cause of proletarian literature, one dedicated to exposing social evil and extolling the virtues of the working and peasant class. This led to verse that was usually accessible, uplifting, and often quite narrative in nature. There the "crisis of language" was diminished by changing the desired effect of poetry: moral and social good, not beauty, was to be its judge. In recent years there has been a radical revision of those poetics, which has given rise to the well-known "misty" (*meng-lung*) poetry. This new poetry reacts against the aesthetics of socialist idealism, creating poetry of indirection, symbolism, and lyricism. While considered avant garde in its immediate context and often criticized for its obscurity and elitism, in the broader context of international modernism this poetry is marked by relative lucidity. What is most remarkable about it is that it seems to rise above May Fourth poetry and to have only a superficial exposure to the classical tradition. Reacting against the poetry (and social conditions) of the last fifty years on the Chinese mainland, it finds company with the new prose fiction and does not suffer from any apparent anxiety caused by its immediate or distant tradition. This may be the result of the extreme changes that Communist rule has brought to the mainland. Poets there write in a context that is relatively tradition-free, and thus they can create more or less out of whole cloth. This has produced some extremely good poetry, which often resembles the imagist verse of the West.

In Taiwan things are very different but strangely parallel. Under the British-American influence, poetry in the 1950s and 1960s was enlisted in the fight against spiritual alienation, which was seen as the inherent modern condition (especially for those exiled in Taiwan). This led to a poetry relatively tortured, difficult, and self-absorbed in nostalgia and sentimentality; the "crisis of language" was solved by pushing the vernacular into realms of obscurity, which aligned the poetry more with European twentieth-century avant garde literary movements. The divorce of this poetry from May Fourth and traditional literature raised significant concerns about its "Chineseness." Works by Hsü Chih-mo and Wen I-to, as well as by Li Po and Tu Fu, were offered for comparison, and most often they seemed to overshadow the later experiments. The arguments that accompanied these developments are emblematic of the problem, as they pit the conservative voice, full of concern for the tradition and fear of innovation, against that of the avant garde poet who cuts a new path but is constantly unsettled by the looming tradition. In the last two decades there has been a slow reappraisal of these arguments, with new aesthetic programs asking for more immediacy and accessibility in poetry. While this has brought some retreat into neoconservative verse, the most interesting and successful new approaches have found accessibility and immediacy in modern voices, including poetry grounded in regional dialects and postmodern play. That there is a strange convergence of the "misty" poetry from the mainland and some recent poetry from Taiwan may be coincidental but significant nonetheless, especially since there is more and more contact between the two groups of poets. While this contact will certainly carry influence both ways across the strait, I believe poetry from Taiwan, with its multiplicity of voices, styles, and subject matter, will exert more influence on the development of mainland poetry in the next twenty years than vice versa. This will be especially so as poets on the mainland move beyond a contemplation of the immediate socio-political conditions with which they have necessarily been preoccupied.

All of these voices in Chinese poetry since 1919 (romanticism, socialism, intellectualism, and the new lyricism) can be seen as valid forms of modernism in the Chinese context. They all wrestle with the disruption that the modern world brought to the Chinese tradition, whether that disruption was political, social, or metaphysical. Yang Mu and Lo Ch'ing inherited those different "modernisms" (in Taiwan, socialism was recast into "regionalism"), integrating them with a command of the tradition that went far beyond that of most of their recent predecessors. They also brought to their poetry a new sense of confidence about their origins and identity. Yang did this as the first important modern poet of Taiwanese heritage, and Lo did so as one of the first mainlanders on Taiwan who was not filled with brooding nostalgia. Yang's personality and training bring to his poetry a blend of the romantic and the intellectual, tempered by his identification with the radical politics of Taiwan. The conceptual complexity and intellectual playfulness of Lo's art, on the other hand, intensify his relatively mainstream personal and academic life.

The use of language is the most obvious point of comparison in the poetries of Yang Mu and Lo Ch'ing. On one level they are, of course, writing in the same language (a modern standard Chinese, what is commonly called Mandarin) and are drawing on and reacting to the same tradition—not only the Chinese but also the Western (particularly English) one. Moreover, Yang and Lo are the products of the same educational system and come from similar social classes. Yang's Taiwanese heritage, which meant that he spoke a Fukienese dialect at home, while extremely important to him personally and to the themes of some of his poetry (see, for example, his "Someone Asked Me about Truth and Justice"), does not seem to have significantly affected his use of language; in this way he is not aligned with the literature of "regionalism." We might also note that Yang speaks a very standard Mandarin. Lo, on the other hand, was raised in and lives in an entirely Mandarin-language environment and his control of the Fukienese dialect is limited. When he wants to bring a certain local flavor to his writing, he does so by employing local expressions common in Taiwan, but this is not important to his use of the language.

The linguistic difference between the two poets is located at the level of diction. There are exceptions, but generally Yang's poetic diction is more elevated, intellectualized, and difficult, while Lo's is relatively simple, filled with everyday expressions and clear syntax. This difference can be partly understood as a function of their ages. Although Yang and Lo were born only eight years apart, their most formative years straddle an important shift in Taiwan's literary world, one in which the intellectualism and obscurity in poetry of the 1960s moved toward the more accessible literature of the 1970s. But beyond these relatively transparent trends (which both poets so easily rise above), there is a fundamental difference in the way their poetries "work." Language is the very vehicle of that difference.

The studied difficulty of Yang's language—from his sophisticated, academic vocabulary to his complex, hypotactic syntax—is one of the most "modern" aspects of his poetry, aligning him with the international modernism of Baudelaire, Rilke, and Eliot. Tempered by a certain amount of romanticism and formalism, Yang

406

may sound most like an early Hart Crane, as is suggested by "After the Snow" (Hsüeh chih):

And after the snow
With cold spreading to the four quarters
I return from the forest
Cannot bear to tread through the myths and poems
Of the courtyard, hesitating still
On the dark and heavy bridge I stand
In the room a lamp burns, and fragments of a song
Seem to come and go wandering slowly on
A potted winter plum lowers its head
Pondering its delicate shadow

A sigh
Seeps out from the double doors
Someone in the room is reading
A slim volume on dream analysis
After the snow, I imagine a fire in the room
And I am the coals of last winter's
Fire, someone igniting me, fanning my flame
A handful of stars murmur in low voices

I must go in
Because I hear that sigh
Like the quiet fragrance of the winter plum seeping through
I hear the turning of pages . . .
Let me analyze your dream
I have returned from afar to give witness to
The disparity in the air temperature between dawn and dusk
And if you are still chilled, you might put
Me into your fireplace, to rekindle
The night's flame

雪止
四處一片寒涼
我自樹林中回來
不忍踏過院子裏的
神話與詩，兀自猶豫
在沉默的橋頭站立
屋裏有燈，彷彿也有
飄零的歌在緩緩游走
一盆臘梅低頭凝視
凝視自己的疏影

我聽見一聲歎息
自重門後傳了過來
有人在屋裏看書
薄薄的一本夢的解析
雪止，我想屋裏也有爐火
而我是去年冬天熄滅的
爐火，有人在點我撥我
一把悉索低語的星子

我不能不向前走
因爲我聽見一聲歎息
像臘梅的香氣暗暗傳來
我聽見翻書的聲音……
你的夢讓我來解析：

我自異鄉回來，爲你印證
晨昏氣溫的差距，若是
你還覺得冷，你不如把我
放進壁爐裏，爲今夜
重新生起一堆火

(*Pei-tou hsing* [Ursa Major], 57–59)

Like much of Yang's work, this poem relies on a slightly archaizing language, one touched with classical phrasing and syntax; the original language of the poem is denser, more formal than this translation can suggest. An educated reader would find this language powerful in its formal control and range of meaning. What the common Chinese reader would find difficult are the ambiguous referents of the poem and the flowing, convoluted syntax.

Although there may be a trend toward simplicity and lucidity in Yang's more recent poetry, particularly that of the early 1980s, linguistic density characterizes much of his work and places it in the center of modern poetry in Taiwan. Yang asks for our undivided attention, expecting us to welcome the opportunity to ponder and plumb the poem for its final referents, for in that activity is the reward of the modern reading experience. Moreover, Yang can at will add layers of allusive material (from a variety of cultural traditions) to a poem to increase this density, which often moves the poem away from romanticism towards intellectualism (see, for example, "Forbidden Games" or "An Autumnal Prayer to Tu Fu").

While much of this linguistic density is available to Lo Ch'ing, he seldom uses it in his poetry (and sometimes offers footnotes when he does). In terms of language, Lo Ch'ing's poetry is surprisingly transparent, although it may be difficult in other areas. Like most classical Chinese poetry, Lo's language is *intended* to be transparent and his syntax balanced and straightforward. There is in this a special appeal to the reader who shies away from the obscure trappings of modernism. Imagine the delight of such a reader upon encountering "A Night on Mount Ah-li" (Ah-li Shan chih yeh):

> The rain has gone by
> The half moon
> Half past midnight
>
> A   few   stars
> Faintly misbehaving
> In the thick clumps of grass
> In the low scattered clouds
> Sliding, running, in and out
>
> Chime, leaving behind
> The sky full of glittering
>   Footsteps
> And the ground covered with sparkling
>   Seeds

雨過

月半

半夜也過

幾顆頑皮的

小，星，星

在深深的草叢裏

在低低的散雲中

溜，進，跑，出

叮叮噹噹的，留下了

滿天眨呀眨的

足音
一地閃閃發光的
種子

(*Ch'ih hsi-kua te fang-fa* [Ways to eat a watermelon], 32–33)

While Lo tends to write short, sometimes epigrammatic poems, in which one might expect this type of language and which will remind the Chinese reader of classical poetry, even his longer poems are built on this linguistic lucidity (see, for example, his structurally complex "On Piscine Metamorphosis").

Along with this lucidity, Lo's poetic language differs from Yang's in its often playful quality, which creates special tensions. The Chinese reader generally expects poetic language to be serious in intent, regardless of its actual form, and thus is quite satisfied with the voice of Yang's poetry; obscure or not, his poems are of high seriousness. Lo's poetry, on the other hand, is full of puns, jokes, and sheer nonsense, lending to it a whimsical, postmodern sense of play. This language play generally does not add to the "thematic significance" of the poem; it is there just for the fun of it. Much of this play is so entrapped in the language that it is untranslatable, but sometimes examples can be rescued. For example, I have translated the dedication to "Raking Leaves" as "For Yang Mu, my rakish host," but actually the pun in Chinese is more complex and nonsensical: punning on Yang's earlier pen name, Yeh Shan (lit., "Leaf/ves Coral"), the dedication reads, "For my raking Leaf/ves Coral host." This certainly does not add anything to the "meaning" of the poem (which is actually quite serious), but rather seems merely to be an occasion for exercising Lo Ch'ing's wit. The accumulation of these occasions throughout his art (his painting is characterized even more by a sense of play) contributes significantly to the humor that is so delightful and distinctive in Lo's poetry, and in the end it helps define his aesthetic vision.

My arrangement of this selection of poetry by Yang and Lo suggests another fundamental difference in their poetic approaches, that is, in the way their poetry establishes larger patterns of meaning. Yang's poetry tends to describe a narrative arc that shadows a biographical line. Lo's, on the other hand, seems to exist in relative stasis, being more conceptual than narrative. We would, of course, be wrong to think that the "life" that we can

410

read out of Yang's poems is the same life as that of the poet/person profiled in this volume. Yet we sense that Yang's poems expect us to see them as moments in *some* life—we want to know the person and circumstances that lie behind the poem. We should think of that life as the persona with the pen names Yeh Shan and Yang Mu, who does not perfectly coincide with the person known as Wang Ching-hsien or C. H. Wang. Doing so, we can then safely speak of the biographical elements in the poetry of Yang Mu. On the other hand, while we might at any given time be able to locate one of Lo Ch'ing's poems in the biography of the person called Lo Ch'ing-che, there is very little in the poetry that asks us to do so; the poem presents itself disencumbered of a historical ego. His poems are somehow twice removed from any narrative event. They are concerned with ideas, theories, speculations, and other abstractions separated from the mundane world. They are not only abiographical, they are often relatively passionless. While Yang's poetry (both as individual poems and as a corpus) describes a narrative line, Lo's tends to fall into groups of contemplations.

When Yang Mu's poem mentions an "I" and a "you," their referents are "real" people who inhabit the world we know—whether they are actual or identifiable people is another question. But when Lo Ch'ing uses personal pronouns, they are often merely rhetorical conveniences. Compare, for example, the opening stanzas of these two poems:

> Here beside the lotus pond
> A bit excited but weary too, we
> Discuss the summer and the direction of the autumn wind
> The sun is bright here beside the lotus pond
> Together we regard how a bird alights on the blossom
> Practicing a bit of the craft of balance and tilt

> 在荷葉的這一邊
> 一些些興奮和倦怠，我們
> 談論著夏天和秋風的方向
> 陽光明亮。在荷葉的這一邊
> 一起觀察飛鳥如何停止在花上
> 學習一些些搖曳和平衡的技巧

("Dance Answers" [Ta wu], *Pei-tou hsing*, 103–105)

Leaning on a pine, I loosen my robe
And sit facing the fresh breeze
Entreating the pine branches and the bright moon
To use the same concern they show the bird's nest
To look after my white-feathered hat flapping to take flight

我就依松解衣

當清風而坐

拜託松枝和明月

用呵護鳥巢的心情

照顧我那振振欲飛的白羽帽子

("If I Had Not Turned into a Pine Tree" [Chia-ju wo mei-yu
pien-ch'eng i-k'o sung-shu], *Shui-tao chih ko* [Rice songs], 99–102)

Despite a number of surface similarities, the implied contexts of
these two poems are dramatically different. The scene around
Yang's lotus pond, whether based on an actual event or not, is one
carved out of the real world and one reconfigured over and over
again in his poetry, from "The River's Edge" (1958) to "Song of
Yesterday's Snow" (1985). This is true even when the poem be-
comes more intellectualized:

This life is long and ongoing this life
You have just begun to comprehend

I explicate a few commonly seen poetic allusions for you
Here beside the lotus pond, sometimes employing the rise and fall
Of history as a metaphor, sometimes the growth and decline
Of living things, sometimes employing
Obscure English terms
Sometimes just silently
Watching you

這一生久遠又長這一生

你剛剛開始察覺到

我為你講解幾個詩詞常見的典故

在荷葉的這一邊，有時以歷史的

興衰為比喻，有時以博物的

榮華頹廢，有時使用

艱深的英文術語

有時靜默

看你

412

As abstract as this conversation sounds, it is one that we keep hearing in Yang's poetry. In "The News" (1958) he says, "And so, we have talked of clouds one hundred seven times"; later, in "Continuing Han Yü's 'Mountain Stones,'" (1968) he says, "After the monk and I discuss the paintings on the temple wall, dawn comes"; and then in "On the Death of a Professor of British Literature" (1977), he remembers "Discussing with me below an oak tree that still dripped with rain / The metaphysical poets." Thus when Yang concludes this "lotus pond" poem by stating, "...allow me / To use the abstract to annotate the concrete / I will not employ any more allusions," we still feel the presence of real people in a real world.

In Lo's poem the clichéd moonlit scene is, however, quickly snatched out of the real world and embedded in one that is abstract and stilled, where the "I," like the moon, pine, and hat, is only a figure of speech. If we try to "biographize" that pronoun, we quickly run into difficulty. The further we go into the poem, the more conceptual this "I" becomes, the following three stanzas reading:

> The moonlight is my mat
> Round stones my pillow
> Porcelain from the Sung holds the wine
> That I drink with T'ang poetry
> To sober up with old romances
>
> And whence I wake
> I find the belt that T'ao Ch'ien dropped
> Lying coiled like a serpentine stream
> With leaves that float on the water
> Forming a school of fish playing beneath the pier
>
> All around the fish
> White clouds rise out of the Han dynasty and
> Silently approach the bank, softly going to drink
> Much like sheep herded by Su Wu on the northern steppes
> Spreading stardust across the sky

我以月光爲席

圓石爲枕

宋瓷盛酒

唐詩下酒

志怪解酒

隨醒之所至
我看到淵明失落的衣帶
成了蜿蜒而去的流水
水中浮沉的落葉
成了戲水釣台的魚群

魚群四周
有白雲從遙遠的漢代浮遊而來
無聲的臨岸，綿綿的聚飲
像極了蘇武牧放的羊群
揚起了一天星星的灰塵

Of course, one could argue that this might be an actual, if somewhat dreamlike, experience of the real world: leaves floating and clouds reflected in the stream intermingle and are transformed by the poet's imagination. Moreover, the easy, tradition-bound imagery of the poem might suggest that we have another reworking of the common "moon, pine, and recluse" theme, in which the poet T'ao Ch'ien is a major figure. Yet the title of Lo's poem should warn us off from any such reading. The concluding stanza drives home the point:

> And still there is the white-feathered hat
> That is actually a white crane—it takes flight and is gone
> Between heaven and earth there remains only one thing
> It is not the recluse in me that has become a pine
> But rather a green pine that has become me

還有那頂白羽帽子
竟真的化成白鶴——　一飛而逝
天地間，唯一留下的
不是一個隱身入青松的我
而是一棵化身爲我的青松

Thus, while Yang Mu filters his personal experience through the language of modernism, Lo Ch'ing draws the traditional imagery of recluse and pine into a new consideration of their theoretical interpenetration.

Many qualities render the poetry of Yang and Lo particularly modern in comparison with their literary heritage, that of both classical poetry and May Fourth literature. In most considerations it is Yang's work that seems the more modern of the two, but on one point his poetry is actually quite traditional (even more so than a great deal of May Fourth poetry): its assumed nonfictional referent. Mainstream classical Chinese poetry is overwhelmingly of this type, and usually is perceived to be built on and celebrating a specific moment in the biography of the poet. In Yang's poetry there are, of course, exceptions (especially where he imitates or engages classical poetry), but generally his poems are ultimately grounded in his everyday world and we are induced to read them as records of actual events. He may venture into the abstract in the course of the poem, but this is usually only to "annotate the concrete." His world is subjective and lyrical, but it is *this* world, and we strive to unravel the poem so that we can see into it. At first reading, one may not be able see that grounding, but if we bore through to the core of the poem, we will find familiar territory. Yang's "Variations on Sorrow: With Key Changes" (Ch'i-liang san fan) offers three scenes that work in this way. The third reads:

> It has not been easy to decipher what your letter
> Really said—I paint a green ridge
> A tumulus, yellow butterflies in swarms
> I paint a white birch there
> A white birch to which the butterflies swarm
>
> Ruminations cause decline
> (Even though it is not the decline of the decline of a
> Nation in grief) I gradually disintegrate, unable
> To stand the wind-eroded loneliness, an abandoned grave
> You want me to keep moving on, on like the trickle of the stream
>
> Someday perhaps you will come by that stream
> Come to this tumulus on the ridge, or perhaps you'll lose your way
> But do not forget that the swarms of butterflies I have painted
> Will lead you to a white birch a foot or so taller than the
> One in the painting. And here I will be . . .

好不容易揣摹你信裏的
意思——我畫一片青山

一座墳，成群黃蝴蝶
我畫一棵白楊樹
蝴蝶飛上白楊樹

疑慮令人衰老
（雖然不如憂國的衰老
衰老）我逐漸解體，但不能
忍受風化的身後蕭條
你要我流動，流動成河流小小

有一天你可以循著河流
來此山中上墳，你或可能迷失
你必須記得我畫過成群的蝴蝶
領你走到一棵比畫中稍高尺許的
白楊樹。我在此……

(*Pei-tou hsing*, 130–31)

While we cannot decipher all the references in this poem, and therein lies part of its strength, still, behind them seems to stand a familiar figure in Yang Mu's poetry: the person abandoned in love. This is not to say that the "meaning" of this, or of any other of Yang's poems is biographical and mundane, but rather that its meaning rises out of the everyday. This is, of course, what the best of classical Chinese poetry does. Tu Fu's "Autumn Meditations" rises directly out of his consideration of everyday K'uei-fu, and Yang's exotic "International Dateline Concerto" is really only his lonely contemplation of the eleven-hours-and-a-day difference that separates Seattle from Taiwan, and him from his new family. While other aspects in these poems might strike the Chinese reader as foreign and difficult, the everyday context of love, family, and separation is extremely welcoming. This familiarity allows Yang to experiment radically in his poetry while retaining the faith of his audience. One example of such experimentation is his use of erotic, sometimes nearly pornographic, language and scenes. In his "Gazing Down," the line "The sun pierces the coolness to illuminate your thighs spread wide" is startling and changes the reading of the rest of the poem, but the poem's world, whether the

416

lithic or carnal, is closer to the traditional vision than that of Lo Ch'ing's poetry.

The level of conceptual abstraction that we find in many of Lo Ch'ing's poems distinguishes them sharply from traditional Chinese poetry, although there are more analogues for this type of abstraction in the poetry of the May Fourth period. Often Lo's poems are built on a metaphor or conceit that overrides or transforms the mundane world. His world is filled with objects that are really ideas, objects that he manipulates in his particularly fertile imagination. In this way his poetry is most like that of Wallace Stevens, although Lo's is certainly less obscure. The objects of which he speaks range from the extremely clichéd of Chinese poetry (moon, mountain, and raft) to the postmodernly bizarre (telephone company advertisements, fluorescent lights, and bird droppings). Reading Lo Ch'ing's poems is often akin to puzzling-out a riddle: we strive to fit the clues together to discover the object or idea that is the "answer" to the poem. We seldom feel that the poetic world that Lo creates is anything like the one in which we pass our everyday lives, and in the context of his tradition this creation of a fictional, cerebral world is Lo's most radical poetic practice. In "The Unsolved Crime" (Hsüan an), Lo actually exposes and comments on his way of writing; included is the answer to the poem's riddle:

The modus operandi of clouds and mist
Is so quick and clean
The scene of the crime is stripped of clues
Leaving behind only an abandoned field
That stares dumbly up at the wide sky
Not knowing what to do—
And the wide sky pretends it has nothing else to do
But to slide slowly on
Toward the north and east, south and west

I heard that this crime was discovered by the sun
Who immediately made certain accusations from the mountain
    ridge
Bringing in the Westville willows for questioning
Interrogating the levees of Southville
Getting the East Branch to give a detailed deposition
Forcing North Isle to explain itself fully and greenly

But after the inquiries were made on all sides
Still a detective as penetrating as the wind

Was at a loss, with no real way to proceed
Nothing to say, no plan of operation
Even if he searched the
Depths of the old forests, the heights of the wild mountains
Still all the clues had vanished, only the consequences remained

"What a mess this is"
"OK, who did it?"
"The mystery man"
"And the suspect?"

To tell the truth
    The whole thing is so nutty
In a word, it was a downpour in the night
When the white punt
Sleeping peacefully in the arms of the dark pool
Along with the stars held within it
Was seduced by the mountain clouds and river mist
And mysteriously disappeared like this

雲霧作案的手法
極爲乾淨俐落
現場，空洞
只留下曠野
不知所措的呆呆仰望著
長天——
而長天卻佯裝無事的
悠悠滑向
　　西　　北　　東　　南

聽說，此案是太陽揭發的
立刻，就在山巔上
提起了公訴：
傳西村之柳，詢南村之堤
套問東江細吐曲折的口供
逼迫北渚詳述青青的自白

然四處奔波打聽之餘
就是精明幹探如風
亦爲之束手，爲之無策
爲之無言而無計可施

即令，搜盡他
莽林百里，荒山千重
依舊是線索全杳，不得要領

　（哎！眞要命）
　（倒底誰，誰）
　（是那謎人的）
　（嫌疑犯呢？）

說起來
　事情可就是這麼絕
總之，才不過半夜急雨
那條酣睡在水塘懷裏的
小白舟
以及舟中一懷的小星星
竟在山雲江霧的誘拐下
如此神秘的——失踪了

(*Ch'ih hsi-kua te fang-fa*, 23–25)

While the surfaces of Lo's poems may make them appear to be rather conventional (as is the landscape imagery of this poem), upon closer inspection, one finds that their spheres of conception make them particularly modern.

As the above remarks suggest, the common thinking that Yang Mu's poetry is obscure and Lo Ch'ing's is transparent is really only half the story. Indeed, Yang Mu's linguistic density contributes to the reader's "difficulty," but his poetry's quotidian grounding also provides some ease. Conversely, Lo Ch'ing's relatively simple language is complicated by abstract conceptual framework, word play (see, for example, "Syllygisms"), or sometimes disturbing vision (in such morbid poems as "Means of Revenge" and "Needlework"). Thus the two poetries offer different reading experiences, but ones that are modern in their "difficulty," for the poetry of modernism is characterized by an assumption that the literary medium (language) is by definition fraught with indeterminacy and subversion.

Yet, in the wide poetic range of these two writers, there are poems that are not modern in this sense. Some of Yang's poetry finds its artistic value in its emotional intensity (and thus is more in line with the reading experience of premodern or classical poetry). The reading of some of Lo Ch'ing's poetry, on the other hand, is located in meaningless word play or in clever ideas. And both men have poems of a more political agenda. The majority of their work is, however, characterized by modern intellectualism and can be analyzed and best appreciated in that light. They seek to create significance in the reading experience, significance that is characterized by the reader's struggle to comprehend, for in that struggle the reader performs the quintessential human activity of making meaning in and out of language. In this poststructuralist world we might argue that the need to create meaning out of language is doomed to failure simply because language is fundamentally unreliable. That is not, however, the modernist argument and in fact it may not matter that this endeavor is doomed to failure. Significance is not created in answering the desire for meaning, but rather in its sheer pursuit. The process is all.

The struggle for meaning in the poetry of Yang Mu and Lo Ch'ing is located at different points in the reading experience. We might say that Yang's poetry is initially difficult and finally easy, while Lo's is the opposite. That is to say, in the reading experience there are two basic steps in the creation of meaning: the reader must first enter into the language of the poem, and then move out of that textual world to the external world to which that language refers. The barriers to meaning lie at both the entry into and exit from the text, and the reader's struggle to overcome those barriers constitutes the bittersweet creation of meaning. Without those barriers the reading experience is without significance. It may be fun, engrossing, or practical, but it is not significantly human.

Generally the barriers that Yang Mu places are in the difficult language that forms the entry into the text. These may be simply technical terms and learned referents, but more often the barrier lies in the language's ambiguity and complexity. This is seen in his ur-modernist poems, such as "Zeelandia" and "Gazing Down," where there is not only lexical difficulty but also syntactic obscurity. The difficulty of his "On a Frosty Night" (Shuang yeh tso) seems to be located solely in this linguistic and syntactic ambiguity:

As if to push back the layers of dead reeds in the final days
	of summer
The aroma of firewood risen from chimneys floats in the air
	with apathy
The breeze comes toward me creeping through this depression,
	a call
Briskly unfolds as if it is inside and outside my eyes,
	duckweed thick
When the hues of remembrance undulate on the tarn, swaying
When the lone long-tailed dragonfly comes flying head on flying
And hesitating, trembling, circling the ripples saturated
	with evening clouds
And designs to alight on the grassy spears that pierce the water
Tapping dust off the still-powdery stamen so that the sunset is
	turned back suddenly
At that instant of change, I push back the layers of dead reeds
As if to push back the layers of dead reeds in those final days of
	summer so far away

I saw, like the soundless scream held by the last dying ashes
In an incense burner before the darkening niche of the spirit's
Idol, enthusiastically elevating that moment to eternal memory
In my own slight discomfort so like a moth beating its
	transparent wings
Against the window outside sequentially rustling parched
	broadleaves like hearts
Turn over in the wind and listlessly drop into the vacant courtyard,
	dark and cool
I saw a band of light from the final days of summer
	on the startled tarn
Lingering, dissolute, chanting deeply an old song intentionally
Turning necessity into coincidence, when the calls of the frogs die
	out one by one
As crickets occupy the wasteland of the young, as I push back the
	dead reeds
And behind them discover time slowly overtaking the final days
	of summer

像撥開重重的蘆葦稈，在夏天末尾
空氣裏飄著柴火穿過煙囪的香氣以淡漠
隨小風向我匍匐的低窪傳來，一種召喚
輕巧地展開又彷彿就在眼瞼裏外，是浮萍擁擠
當水塘上鼓盪片段緬懷的色彩，搖擺著
當孤單的長尾蜻蜓從正前方飛來飛來
猶豫抖動，盤旋於吸納了充份霞光的漣漪

並且試圖在穎豎的一根刺水芒草上小駐
點碎了粉末般的花蕊致使暮色折回那遽然
變化的時刻，我撥開重重的蘆葦稈當我
像撥開重重的蘆葦稈在那遙遠的夏天的末尾

我看到，一如香爐上最後熄滅的灰燼
在已然暗將下來的神龕前堅持著無聲的
吶喊，努力將那瞬息提升爲永恆的記憶
在我輕微的不安裏如蛾拍打透明的翼
窗外陸續吹響一些乾燥的闊葉，像心臟
在風裏轉動遂茫茫墜落空洞的庭院，陰涼
我看到夏天末尾一片光明在驚悸的水塘上
流連不去，閒散，低吟著漫長的古歌有意
將一切必然化爲偶然，在蛙鳴次第寂寞的時候
當蟋蟀全面佔領了童年的荒郊，當我撥開蘆葦稈
向前並且發現時光正在慢慢超越那夏天的末尾

(*Yu-jen* [Someone], 30–32)

There is a nearly visceral delight in pushing one's way through the dense language of such a poem (and the language is certainly richer and more difficult in the original). Phrases intersect and words flutter in indeterminacy, caught between one point of reference and another. We are constantly revising our reading as we read, careful not to deny the possibilities of the words, letting the multiple meanings accrue as we go. Yet all this textual pleasure is sustained by knowing, or at least hoping, that we, too, in the end can see through the reeds to the mundane world of which Yang writes. We have faith that if we read well, we will be rewarded with a sense of the human, we will be able to share with him a world full-blooded and essentially alive. Indeterminacy will momentarily be held at bay. It is the possibility of easy exit that sustains our reading. If we remain trapped within the text, for whatever reason, then our pleasure turns to frustration and the reading experience fails to bring us to significance. If that happens too often we will lose faith in the text or in our ability to read it, and we will stop reading altogether.

In Lo Ch'ing's poetry the reader generally enters the textual world easily, sliding effortlessly through its open, porous text, welcomed by its simple language and encouraged to linger in its straightforward syntax. But if the reader is allowed to leave the text as effortlessly, and is not asked at some point to contribute to its creation, that, too, is a failed reading experience. Certainly this is not the case with Lo's "Landscape on a Jar" (Hu chung shan-shui):

Delicately painting the spring rain on a porcelain jar
And placing it carefully on a hill in summer
Painting the landscape and jar together
On a tiny autumnal fan

Just now
The snowscape that wasn't painted on the fan
Unexpectedly, so very clearly
Appears on the porcelain jar

And what gathers on the jar
Is undoubtedly
All the spring rains
Of the world

把春水細細畫在瓷壺上
把瓷壺穩穩放在夏山中
再把山水瓷壺一起畫入
一把小小的秋扇裏

就在這個時候
那沒有畫進扇面的雪景
竟然清清楚楚的
出現在瓷壺之上

而壺中所聚的
當然是
天下所有的
春水

(*Pu-ming fei-hsing-wu lai-le* [Here come the UFOs], 94)

The lucidity of the language and referents here, simple objects found in so many traditional Chinese poems, belies the conceptional difficulty of the poem. If we are not careful, we will pass too easily through the reading experience, sliding out of the poem into our mundane world without realizing that the world Lo creates in the poem is strangely at odds with our own. In its easy phrasing we might fail to notice that the poem produces a complex transformation of landscapes, jars, and spring rains, such that when we try to decipher the referentiality of the poem we are stymied by the paradox of the poet's vision. We cannot determine, for example, on which jar the snow falls: the one on which the landscape is painted, or the one that is painted (along with its painted landscape) on the autumnal fan. The process of transformation and replacement that underlies this conception is fundamental to Lo's poetics. While Yang Mu builds a world of multiple referents that exist simultaneously in the reader's consideration, Lo builds his poems on self-extinguishing transformations: X becomes Y, Y becomes Z, and Z strangely becomes A. Lo uses several grammatical and rhetorical patterns to accomplish those transformations; often this is a simple grammatical device that adds a resultative ending (*ch'eng*) to a transitive verb, producing "X is *verbed* into Y." In everyday speech we see this commonly in such compounds as *tso-ch'eng* (made into) and *fan-ch'eng* (translate into). Lo uses many of these conventional forms, but he also expands the pattern to include such neologisms as " . . . swaying himself into [*yao-ch'eng*] / Its first barren tree" ("The Curious Arhat," in "Bizarre Manifestations of the Dharma") and "Raking our way into [*sao-ch'eng*] 'Raking Leaves in the Dusk,' a sketch done in gray washes" ("Raking Leaves").

Just as we must have faith that behind Yang Mu's smoke screen of language there is a world that we understand, with Lo's poetry we must *doubt* the lucidity of the text. We must be induced to ponder its simplicity, assuming that its meaning is more than its immediate referent. We wonder what, after all, is the ladder on the wall, the goldfish in the pond, the crow in his cage. We come to that fruitful state of doubt by repeatedly finding meaning where there seemingly is none. Again and again, nothing is transformed into something. In that struggle to create meaning out of the meaningless, even if we fail, we find ourselves participating in the essentially human task of making sense of the world of/in words.

The poetry of both Yang Mu and Lo Ch'ing is rich and multifaceted; for every type of poem I have offered here as representative of their art, there is at least one, even in this small selection, that can be offered as a counterexample. I argue that Yang's poetry is grounded in the everyday while Lo's is more conceptual, but there are also Yang's "Cicada" and "Spring Song" and Lo's "Fluorescent Lights" and "The Sound of a Motor Coming from Afar" to prove me wrong. While we expect the language of Yang's poetry to be more difficult than Lo's, still there are the important poems "Someone Asked Me about Truth and Justice" and "The Avenging Ghost," in which this is not true. Yet in all their complexity there is still a consistency of vision within the poetry of each poet that we recognize and come to expect.

That consistency is related directly to the two poets' training and professional work, as well as to their personalities. Perhaps most consistent in Yang's poetry is its high sense of seriousness; whether in a purely lyrical mode, in one of intense intertextuality, or one filled with political comment, the poem is always a sober exploration of the real and literary worlds. The many facets of the poem, both in theme and form, combine to yield a mature and unified consideration of its subject. Since Yang has spent much of his academic life considering and explicating classical, primarily (but not exclusively) Chinese, poetry, we can understand the seriousness he brings to his own writing. In his academic writings, which rely on close readings tempered by Chinese philology, Yang probes the texts, extracting new readings that are always well argued and logically unified. When he turns to his creative writing, he brings those qualities with him. In "Continuing Han Yü's 'Mountain Stones,'" for example, Yang welds the seriousness of the classical tradition with his own lyrical intensity, while in "Zeelandia" the history of imperialism in Taiwan is integrated with an eroticized moment in the present. Yang may ground his poems in the everyday world, but they are not occasional verses that he writes as social discourse. For Yang, poetry is a serious, ordered, and life-sustaining activity. It is his way of not only capturing the moment, but of moving that moment onto a higher level of significance.

While Lo Ch'ing certainly feels that art is a serious endeavor, his work is more likely to experiment with the unconventional and humorous. He creates works that are unified on a conceptual level but often are constructed out of seemingly heterogeneous parts. The most extreme examples are his "Waking the Sleeping Dragon," which uses the language of *kung-fu* pulp fiction to discuss art and innovation, and his "A Good-bye Epistle about Good-bye," which appears to be pure postmodern word play constructed out of conventional epistolary salutations and closings. This approach to art may be primarily a result of Lo's personal circumstances, but it also seems to be related to his training as a painter, especially as he has developed an artistic style that derives from the Ming eccentrics and unorthodox Zen painters, who delight in the incongruous and bizarre. Lo has many serious, more conventional poems, and his academic writing can also be of that type, but I would argue that the intellectual process that best informs his poetry derives from his painterly life.

To illustrate the different aesthetic rationales that underlie the poetries of Yang Mu and Lo Ch'ing we might consider their poetic sequences. In this volume we have four full sequences by Yang (along with selections from others) and five by Lo. Of those, the two earliest (Yang's "King Wu's Encampment: A Suite of Songs" and Lo's "Six Ways to Eat a Watermelon") are perhaps most revealing of their poetic approaches. First we should consider their titles. Yang's title derives from the oldest and most revered poetic text in China, *The Book of Songs,* and thus announces its intimate relationship with the tradition and its serious intent: King Wu's military exploits are part of what Yang identifies as the Chinese epic, *The Weniad* (a sequence of five poems from *The Book of Songs),* which is mentioned in the illustrative text to that section of poems. While the subtitle reinforces the seriousness of the poems, as well as suggests the nature of their sequential relationship, it also identifies the poems as cosmopolitan in their modernity (the term "suite" [*tsu ch'ü*] is used only for Western musical works). Similar musical designations ("rondo," "concerto") appear in other sequences by Yang. Lo Ch'ing's title, on the other hand, has absolutely no serious, traditional, or cosmopolitan overtones; it is just plain funny. What could be easier than eating watermelon? (All you have to do is decide whether to spit out the seeds or swallow them.) We need six ways? Lo's title sounds like eating instructions in a guidebook for an alien tourist. This sense of the absurd is continued in the titles for the individual poems (note that in "King Wu's Encampment" Yang uses chaste Arabic numerals), where the staid and mundane meet in a bizarre incongruity.

The announced seriousness of Yang's sequence is reinforced by the sobriety of his language, which is not overly obscure but appropriately arcane and allusive. From the archaic dating in the first poem to a metonymic reference to the Chou state (the ancient capital sites) and embedded quotations ("so shall you reap") of the second, we proceed relatively slowly and deliberately through the sequence. To these references Yang adds a shifting point of view and cryptic references, particularly in the third poem: the "ford" must be at Meng-chin and the "western land" is probably the original city-state of Chou, but what are the "elegant debates" and who are "you" and the "widows"? These are much less certain. The language in Lo Ch'ing's "Watermelon" sequence is clean, mechanical, and allusionless. Where it calls attention to itself is in its rather nonsensical flourishes. For example, the closing of "The Fifth Way" (i.e., the first poem in the sequence) is built upon the simple grammatical construction "A *ken* b *i-yang*" (A and B are alike), but in this rendering the "ands" (*ken*) pile up unnaturally and the word *i-yang* is on a separate line with its two syllables split by a comma, which I translate as "A/Like." Thus, Yang's language keeps asking us to look deeper into the text for more clues to its meaning, while Lo's reminds us of the apparent absurdity of the sequence.

Throughout Yang's poem we sense a depth of meaning. The text seems to be composed of layers of reference, some of which are apparent, and others that may always be hidden. Although this does not seem to be the case here, Yang's poems often fuse several points of view, events, and times together is a single consideration. This is obvious in "The International Dateline Concerto" and "Gazing Down," and elsewhere is likely to be so; the "Forbidden Game" sequence seems to meld present-day Granada with the Granada of Lorca's life. In those poems the untangling of the multiple points of reference is an essential part of the reading act. It is also a gradual act that, in the best of Yang's poems, never is finished (he seems to make sure that the threads can never be completely untangled). In the end, however, we return to some semblance of order and understanding. So it is with his "King Wu" sequence. While we may not be able to account for all the elements, with the proper probing we can build the narrative that lies behind Yang's poem, and it is a simple, but momentous story. King Wu, the martial king, kills his own sovereign to establish the first real Chinese state; thus Chinese civilization is built on the legacy of regicide. This was perhaps necessary and ultimately good, but, under the circumstances, we should "prepare no robes no wine for the victors who come home this time." Years later Yang would retell that narrative and its accompanying lesson in his academic reconstruction of *The Weniad*. That he himself had earlier traced that narrative in his own sequence is a testimony to his creative vision.

How different is the structure of Lo Ch'ing's "Watermelon" sequence. The poems certainly do not tell a story; if anything they are more like a series of thoughts on the watermelon as an idea, and a weird idea at that. We do not move slowly through the text deciphering its images; rather, if there is "understanding" at all, it comes in bursts, a modern form of Zen's "instant enlightenment" —a verbal whack on the head. If there is an informing discourse behind the series, it is not the intellectual probing of the academic essay, but rather something akin to the leaves of a Chinese album painting: a series of slightly quizzical renderings of the watermelon in various poses. We know, for instance, that the "Bizarre Manifestations of the Dharma" sequence also exists as a series of album paintings: why not these watermelons too? But of course the sequence here is numbered *backwards* and the sixth poem is missing completely. If we are looking for the final unity that we find in Yang's poetry, we are certainly out of luck with Lo. The series itself is not even whole. But where is that last poem? Perhaps it is waiting for us to finish the first poem, but, as the title says (and we have only the title) we must eat first. Surprisingly, this sequence was one of Lo Ch'ing's earliest publications (and many readers still know him principally by it). It is particularly fitting that Lo's reputation was established by a poem he never wrote. In the 1980s he would discover and become infatuated with the word and world of postmodernism. Yet years before, he had already spoken in its voice; this, too, is testimony to his poetic genius.

Sources

Yang Mu

Chin-chi te yu-hsi (Forbidden games): Cicada; Forbidden Games; On the Death of a Professor of British Literature

Hai-an ch'i-tieh (Seven islands along the coast): Conversation Class; Fourteen Sonnets for Ming-ming; The International Dateline Concerto

Pei-tou hsing (Ursa Major): After the Snow; Dance Answers; Kaohsiung; A Love Poem; Solitude; A Stand of Reeds; A Stand of Rice; Variations on Sorrow: With Key Changes; What Is in Your Heart; Zeelandia

Yang Mu shih-chi: 1 (The collected poems of Yang Mu, vol. 1): April 2: With Yu Kwang-chung Watching the Michigan Snow Melt; An Autumnal Prayer to Tu Fu; Bring on the Wine; Continuing Han Yü's "Mountain Stones"; In the Cornfields of the Dark Night; King Wu's Encampment: A Suite of Songs; The News; A Ranch in the Rain; The River's Edge; A Set of Fourteen Sonnets; Six Songs to the Tune "Partridge Skies"; Summertime; Surprise Lilies; The Town Where You Live; When the Wind Comes Up; The Wind Rolls through the Snowy Woods

Yu-jen (Someone): Gazing Down; Moon over Pass Mountain; On a Frosty Night; The Panjshir Valley; Someone Asked Me about Truth and Justice; Song of Yesterday's Snow; Spring Song

Lo Ch'ing

Ch'ih hsi-kua te fang-fa (Ways to eat a watermelon): The House; Means of Revenge; A Night on Mount Ah-li; Ode to the Southwest Wind; Six Ways to Eat a Watermelon; Syllygisms; The Teacup Theorems; Two Trees; The Unsolved Crime

Cho-tsei chi (To catch a thief): Art Appreciation; The Avenging Ghost; Bitter Tea; Book Burning; The Invisible Man; Metamorphosis; Needlework; A Night on Mount Pleiades; On Piscine Metamorphosis; Raking Leaves; Reading Paintings in the Cloud-Nourishing Studio; Self-Sacrifice; A Silent Prayer

Lu ying shih-hsüeh (Video poetics): Fluorescent Lights; A Good-bye Epistle about Good-bye; Hey, What's Up?; The Little Commander of Donkeys; Once More Looking out at the Deep Blue Sea after Looking out at the Deep Blue Sea Many Times Before; Saddle Vine; Sunrise

Pu-ming fei-hsing-wu lai-le (Here come the UFOs): Bizarre Manifestations of the Dharma; Found by the Pool; Into Autumn: Eighteen Lines;

Bibliography of Selected Works by Yang Mu and Lo Ch'ing

Yang Mu

Books in Chinese (excluding volumes edited by Yang Mu)

Chiao-liu tao (By way of exchange). Taipei: Hung-fan, 1985. Commentary.

Chin-chi te yu-hsi (Forbidden games). Taipei: Hung-fan, 1980. Poetry.

Ch'uan-shuo (Legends). Taipei: Chih-wen, 1971. Poetry.

Ch'uan-t'ung-te yü hsien-tai-te (The traditional and the modern). Taipei: Chih-wen, 1974. Criticism.

Fei-kuo huo-shan (Volcano fly-by). Taipei: Hung-fan, 1986. Commentary.

Hai-an ch'i-tieh (Seven islands along the coast). Taipei: Hung-fan, 1980. Poetry.

Hua chi (The flower season). Taipei: Lan-hsing, 1963. Poetry.

I-shou shih te wan-ch'eng (The completion of a poem). Taipei: Hung-fan, 1989. Essays.

Lu Chi "Wen-fu" chiao-shih (An annotated edition of Lu Chi's "Rhapsody on Literature"). Taipei: Hung-fan, 1985.

Nien lun (The annual cycle). Taipei: Hung-fan, 1976. Essay.

Pei-tou hsing (Ursa Major). Taipei: Hung-fan, 1978. Poetry.

P'ing chung kao (Manuscript in a bottle). Taipei: Chih-wen, 1975. Poetry.

Po-k'o-lai ching-shen (The spirit of Berkeley). Taipei: Hung-fan, 1977. Essays.

Shan-feng hai-yü (Mountain winds and ocean rains). Taipei: Hung-fan, 1987. Memoir.

Shui chih mei (The river's edge). Taipei: Lan-hsing, 1960. Poetry.

Sou-suo-che (The searcher). Taipei: Hung-fan, 1982. Essays.

Teng-ch'uan (Lantern boat). Taipei: Wen-hsing, 1966. Poetry.

Wan-cheng te yü-yen (The complete fable). Taipei: Hung-fan, 1991. Poetry.

Wen-hsüeh chih-shih (Literary knowledge). Taipei: Hung-fan, 1979. Criticism.

Wen-hsüeh te yüan-liu (The origins of literature). Taipei: Hung-fan, 1984. Criticism.

Wu Feng. (Wu Feng). Taipei: Hung-fan, 1979. Drama in verse.

Yang Mu shih-chi. I: 1956–1974 (The collected poems of Yang Mu. Vol. I: 1956–1974). Taipei: Hung-fan, 1978.

Yeh Shan san-wen chi (The collected essays of Yeh Shan), Taipei: Wen-hsing, 1966.

Yu-jen (Someone). Taipei: Hung-fan, 1986. Poetry.

Books in English

The Bell and the Drum: Shih Ching as Formulaic Poetry in an Oral Tradition. Berkeley: University of California Press, 1974.

From Ritual to Allegory: Seven Essays in Early Chinese Poetry. Hong Kong: Chinese University Press, 1988.

Lo Ch'ing

Books in Chinese (excluding volumes edited by Lo Ch'ing)

Ch'ih hsi-kua te fang-fa (Ways to eat a watermelon). Taipei: Yu-shih, 1972. Poetry.

Cho-tsei chi (To catch a thief). Taipei: Hung-fan, 1977. Poetry.

Lo Ch'ing san-wen chi (The collected essays of Lo Ch'ing). Taipei: Hung-fan, 1976.

Lu-ying shih-hsüeh (Video poetics). Taipei: Shu-lin, 1988. Poetry.

Pu-ming fei-hsing-wu lai-le (Here come the UFOs). Taipei: Ch'ung-wen, 1984. Paintings and poetry.

Shen-chou hao-hsia chuan (The gallant knight of Cathay). Taipei: Wu-ling, 1975. Poetry.

Shen-ma shih hou-hsien-tai chu-i? (What is postmodernism?). Taipei: Shu-lin, 1989. Criticism.

Shih-jen chih ch'iao (The poet's bridge). Taipei: Wu-ssu, 1988. Criticism.

Shih-jen chih teng (The poet's lamp). Taipei: Kuang-fu, 1988. Essays.

Shui-mo chih mei (The aesthetics of ink). Taipei: Yu-shih, 1991. Art criticism.

Shui-tao chih ko (Rice songs). Taipei: Ta-ti, 1981. Poetry.

Ts'ung Hsü Chih-mo tao Yü Kuang-chung (From Hsü Chih-mo to Yu Kwang-chung). Taipei: Erh-ya, 1978. Criticism.

Ying-huo ch'ung (Firefly). Taipei: Taiwan sheng chiao-yü, 1987. Paintings and poetry for children.

Major Recent Exhibitions

Find the Recluse: One Man Exhibition. Lady David Art Gallery, Percival David Foundation of Chinese Art, London, July 5–August 3, 1990.

The Beijing Modern Chinese Painting Exhibition (works by twelve painters), Beijing Fine Arts Museum, Beijing, 1988.

The Second Annual Chinese Painting Exhibition (prize winning). Lion Gallery, Taipei, 1988.

Young Artists in Taiwan: Exhibition of Chinese Ink Painting, Oil Painting, Watercolor and Graphic Arts. East-West Center, Honolulu, January 11–March 13, 1987.

A Semiology of Painting: An Exhibition of Lo Ch'ing's Ink Paintings. Caves Gallery, Taipei, January 3–15, 1986.

China, China, Poetry and Painting of the Republic of China. Brussels, 1986.

Chinese Painting by Lo Ch'ing. Chinatown Cultural Service Center, New York State Council of the Arts, New York, 1986.

The Twenty-second Annual Modern Art of Asia Exhibition (special award). Tokyo, 1986.

Lo Ch'ing's Ink Painting: An Exhibit. Avant Garde Art Center, Taichung, Taiwan, June 22—30, 1985.

An Exhibition of Chinese Ink Paintings by Lo Ch'ing. Yü Shu-fang Gallery, Kaohsiung, Taiwan, March 2—15, 1984.

Two contemporary poets from Taiwan, Yang Mu (pen name for Wang Ching-hsien, b. 1940) and Lo Ch'ing (pen name for Lo Ch'ing-che, b. 1948), are represented in this bilingual edition of Chinese poetry ranging from the romantic to the postmodern. Both poets were involved in the selection of poems for this volume, the first edition in any language of their selected work. Their backgrounds, literary styles, and professional lives are profiled and compared by translator Joseph R. Allen in critical essays that show how Yang and Lo represent basic directions in modern Chinese poetics and how they have contributed to the definition of modernism and postmodernism in China.

The book's organization reflects each poet's method of composition. Yang's poems are chronologically arranged, as his poetry tends to describe a narrative line that closely parallels his own biography. Lo's poems, which explore a world of concept and metaphor, are grouped by theme. Although each poet has a range of poetic voices, Yang's work can be considered the peak of high modernism in Chinese poetry, while Lo's more problematic work suggests the direction of new explorations in the art. In this way the two poets are mutually illuminating.

Each group of poems is prefaced by an "illustration" that draws from another side of the poet's intellectual life. For Yang, who is a professor of comparative literature at the University of Washington, these are excerpts from his academic work (written under the name C. H. Wang) in English. The poems by Lo, a well-known painter living in Taiwan, are illustrated by five of his own ink paintings.

Joseph R. Allen is associate professor of Chinese language and literature at Washington University, St. Louis. He is the author of *In the Voice of Others: Chinese Music Bureau Poetry*.